T0050559

Unrepentant

Disrobing the Emperor

Unrepentant

Disrobing the Emperor

Kevin Annett

BOOKS

Winchester, UK
Washington, USA

First published by O-Books, 2010
O Books is an imprint of John Hunt Publishing Ltd., The Bothy, Deershot Lodge, Park Lane, Ropley,
Hants, SO24 OBE, UK
office1@o-books.net
www.o-books.com

Distribution in:	South Africa
	Stephan Phillips (pty) Ltd
UK and Europe	Email: orders@stephanphillips.com
Orca Book Services Ltd	Tel: 27 21 4489839 Telefax: 27 21 4479879
Home trade orders	Text copyright Kevin Annett 2010
tradeorders@orcabookservices.co.uk	
Tel: 01235 465521 Fax: 01235 465555	ISBN: 978 1 84694 405 5
Export orders	Design: Tom Davies
exportorders@orcabookservices.co.uk	
Tel: 01235 465516 or 01235 465517	All rights reserved. Except for brief quotations
Fax: 01235 465555	in critical articles or reviews, no part of this
	book may be reproduced in any manner
USA and Canada	without prior written permission from the
NBN	publishers.
custserv@nbnbooks.com	
Tel: 1 800 462 6420 Fax: 1 800 338 4550	The rights of Kevin Annett as author have been
	asserted in accordance with the Copyright,
Australia and New Zealand	Designs and Patents Act 1988.
Brumby Books	
sales@brumbybooks.com.au	A CIP catalogue record for this book is
Tel: 61 3 9761 5535 Fax: 61 3 9761 7095	available from the British Library.
Far East (offices in Singapore, Thailand,	
Hong Kong, Taiwan)	
Pansing Distribution Pte Ltd	
kemal@pansing.com	
Tel: 65 6319 9939 Fax: 65 6462 5761	Printed in the UK by CPI Antony Rowe

We operate a distinctive and ethical publishing philosophy in all
areas of its business, from its global network of authors to
production and worldwide distribution.

CONTENTS

This book is dedicated to the survivors,
and to the children who died

Under a regime where murder is officially sanctioned, there can be no regret and no apology.
Simon Wiesenthal

Foreword

The whites told only one side. Told it to please themselves. Told much that is not true. Only his best deeds, only the worse deeds of the Indians, has the white man told.
Yellow Wolf, Nez Perce, 1856–1935

The facts affirmed in this book will seem strange to students grounded in traditional lore. Some persons may find it incredible that the righteous, god-fearing folk who were their ancestors could have engaged in such practices as are here described, especially the pervasive calculated deception of the official records ... Persons and groups reaching for illicit power customarily assume attitudes of great moral rectitude to divert attention from the abandonment of their own moral standards of behavior.
Frederick Turner, *Beyond Geography*

My mother tried her best to take the 'savage' out of me, mainly because of the extreme prejudice that her father had suffered. So at six years old I was sent to Sunday school. I hated it! After several months of attending, we were being read, as I remember it, from one of the books of Kings. In the story God sweeps down upon some city that he is unhappy with and smites the entire citizenry: men, women, and children. It immediately dawns on me that God is not as good or as fair as my own earthly father, so why did He deserve my obedience and worship? That was the last day that I attended Sunday school. However, it left a lasting impression on me.

I was so influenced by my grandfather that I knew that even a chief had no power over any individual's decision. It was always, for instance, a warrior's choice to go to war. If a warrior believed that a war was not justified, he simply chose not to partake in it. This may not have been true of all tribes, particularly in the Northwest, but it was from my grandfather's Nanticoke and Lakota heritage.

As my education and reading progressed it became evident that White (a culture, not a race) Civilization existed on the sorrow and pain of those who were not White or Civilized. It was clear that colonial powers wanted only one thing from those whose lands they invaded, not 'discovered': their resources, whether they were human bodies or land or gold, or in more modern times oil and metals. The story was always the same: 'We are bringing you a better way of life; we are bringing you salvation through Jesus; we are bringing you law and government.' No matter the gift, it is always an agenda of power and more resources for the Great White Father (the secular God) and physical and cultural genocide for the indigenous peoples living there.

The words of Commissioner of Indian Affairs, Francis Walker, say it all; he wrote in 1872:

'There is no question of national dignity ... involved in the treatment of savages by a civilized power.'

Later, he said that he and his people could reduce 'the wild beasts to the condition of the supplicants of charity' by the use of reservations, or ghettos in other places. This was true whether the scene was North America, South America, Africa, or any other place the White Man 'discovered'.

The Christians had the backing of God and Scripture in their justification of the taking of Indian land and lives, witness two favorites of the Puritans:

Ask of me, and I shall give thee the heathen for thine inheritance, and the uttermost parts of the earth for thy possession.
(Psalm 2:8, Authorized Version)

And

> 'Whosoever therefore resisteth the power, resisteth the ordinance of God: and they that resist shall receive to themselves damnation'
> (Romans 13:2, AV).

In short, the Civilized White Man believed, and still does, that he has the right to the land, the resources, and the lives of those who are not White, Christian, or Civilized. And often the children are a main target, for, as General Sherman said, 'Nits become lice.' As the Tsististas (Cheyenne) Roxanne Dunbar Ortiz put it in 1938, 'Genocide is a colonial policy, not an accident.'

This is only background to the subject at hand: the residential schools in Canada. Not surprisingly, the torture and death that these schools brought to the children of Indian tribes have long been common in the United States and were even written about early in the twentieth century by Chief Luther Standing Bear and others. Standing Bear talks of the same mortality rate at the Carlisle Indian School in Carlisle, Pennsylvania as Kevin Annett speaks of in Canada – 50%.

In the mid-1990s Reverend Kevin Annett accepted a position in Port Alberni on Vancouver Island at St Andrew's, a parish consisting mostly of the old guard of that town. Kevin's trouble began with an innocent enough question, 'Why are there not any Indians in our congregation?' It was the wrong question to ask and began his 'downfall' or rather his becoming a warrior in the truest sense of the word.

This is the story of one man who loses all, is reduced to poverty, and whose very name is revulsion to others. This man locks horns with the two greatest civilized instruments of power – the state and the church and, behind them, willing to do their bidding like a Nazi elite guard, stand the Royal Canadian Mounted Police and a coterie of thugs. This man takes on the most dangerous of all tasks: fighting the organized power of church and state.

We have seen what happens to people like that, from Socrates, to Jesus, to Bruno, to Martin Luther King Jr. The odds of winning are slim to almost nothing. So, here we have a man who seeks both justice and the truth, whose life is constantly at stake, for doing what a human being is supposed to do: help the helpless, speak the truth, and seek what is fair and noble.

Among these great individuals, and Kevin Annett is among them, he is no less than a *hero*.

What Kevin discovers and documents as having gone on at the Canadian residential schools for Indian children are not only crimes, for 'crime' is a legal word of the state and many 'crimes' are permitted to exist, such as refusing to kill innocent people and children in warfare. There are abuses that go far deeper even than 'crimes against humanity'. These are crimes against our very soul, against what it is to be a human being, against all that has been held sacred by humankind for a million years. Beyond crime, it is psychopathology at its worst.

When I was about eight years old my grandfather said to me, 'Kurt, there is all the difference in the world between a civilized person and a human being.' And in conversation, Fools Crow, the last of the Oglala Lakota ceremonial chiefs, and the greatest medicine man of the twentieth century, said, 'The White Man is a mutant.' It is the word that I have come to use to distinguish between civilized man and natural, tribal man and prehistoric man.

The mutants of greed, gluttony, power, self-centeredness, and empty souls are in charge here, not Jesus, not Gandhi, not the human genome, not our human history before civilization or among the uncivilized, for the most part. So, what Kevin Annett reports is not just the story of the churches, the state, the educational system, but the story of civilized man, of us!

One example is germane to the topic of Kevin's book – the

genocide, and its subsequent hiding, of thousands of Native Americans at the hands of the churches and the state: the two quintessential powers for the past 2,000 years. Remember, these are children, children who have nails driven through their tongues for speaking their own language.

These mutant-type activities and beliefs raise children in opposition to their genetic make-up, to their genome. All of this is abuse and the proof is in the pudding – a society of self-centered people, massive numbers suffering from depression and persistent anxiety, fear, the constant drugging of the individual with TV, amusement, sex, and the consumption of objects, a hatred of the Other, be it Nature or people. What is important is that the things mentioned are not merely self-destructive, they are parent-destructive; they destroy the natural and genetic programs we all have to be good, life-enhancing parents.

Civilized man perhaps more than in any other way displays his 'mutancy' and wayward development from the genetic and former cultural structures of the human being, thus rendering himself pathological. The residential schools are just one of many examples of this.

The following statements were made by those who lived with their counterparts and, non-civilized themselves, were Real Human Beings:

If you do bad things your children will follow you and do the same. If you want to raise good children be decent yourself.
(In-The-Middle, Mescalero Apache)

Good acts done for the love of children become stories good for the ears of people from other bands; they become as coveted things.
(Social tradition, Assiniboine)

We do not want riches, but we want to train our children right
… We want peace and love.
(Red Cloud, Oglala Lakota)

The following is from Chief Luther Standing Bear's account of his childhood:

> As the Lakota child developed, it had the constant companionship of an elder; if not father or mother, then aunt, uncle or one of the numerous cousins of the band. Children were always welcome charges of all who were older. Every child not only belonged to a certain family, but also belonged to the band, and no matter where it strayed when it was able to walk, it was at home, for everyone in the band claimed relationship.

> In manner, gentleness was my mother's outstanding characteristic. Never did she, nor any of my caretakers, ever speak crossly to me or scold me for failures or shortcomings. For an elder person in the Lakota tribe to strike or punish a young person was an intolerable brutality. Such an ugly thing as force with anger back of it was unknown to me, for it was never exhibited in my presence.

True Indian education was based on the development of individual qualities and recognition of rights. Native education was not a class education but one that strengthened and encouraged the individual to grow. So if today I had a young mind to direct, to start on the journey of life, and I was faced with the duty of choosing between the natural way of my forefathers and that of the White Man's present way of civilization, I would unhesitatingly set that child's feet in the path of my forefathers. I would raise him or her to be an Indian!

The mutant was not a mutant prior to his/her birth. He/she

was made one because its culture and its parents refused to love it, no matter how well they think they tried. Here is the wisdom of the great twentieth-century anthropologist Ashley Montagu:

> The newborn by its evolutionary genetic structure expects to be held and touched the moment she is born. This need to have skin to skin contact with her mother is so important the first three or more years of life, and even through adulthood, that those who are deprived of it very often cannot fully give or love as an adult ... They find it hard to give the very thing that they were deprived of: affectionate touch and selfless love. They may succeed very well in the world, but they will seldom if ever experience deep joy ... They consider a good relationship one in which they have fun and does not demand or expect affection or the expression of tender emotions.

When we leave this Earth only two things will remain: our love and our abuse, and both will flow through to the coming generations either for better or for worse. So far it has been for worse. Perhaps the mothers of the world can improve on our history.

Kurt Kaltreider PhD

Kurt Kaltreider is of Nanticoke/Lakota and German/English descent. He graduated from Gettysburg College and holds an MA and PhD in philosophy and clinical psychology from the University of Tennessee. He has written two books on native culture and has devoted his life to the protection and support of the ways of his ancestors. He lives in Ashland, Oregon.

Prologue
When Churchyards Yawn

The years have hidden most of their features now, covering the truth with blackberry brambles, towering maples or elms, and often hurriedly piled soil. But like the shell holes of forgotten wars, the mass graves that dot our landscape tell those who will learn, about what really happened in the cold and deadly halls of the Indian residential schools.

Children were buried in these places. Many children.

Tuberculosis-ridden, or beaten featureless, their little bodies were dumped in these places in the pit of night. The youngest victims were newborn babies, born of rape at the hands of men who wore crosses and spoke of God. Sometimes, fearing the evidence of their crime, they burned their children in the school furnaces. Some of them undoubtedly said a prayer when they did so. Other children looked on, or held the furnace door open, and speak today of what they saw.

Maisie Shaw. Elaine Dick. Maggie Seward. Richard Thomas. Vicky Stewart. Albert Cardinal. Margaret Sepass. George Spuzzum. Denis Albert. Albert Hance. Joseph Jones. Francis Webster. Sandy Mitchell. John Charlie. Mitchell Joseph. Bernadette Thomas. Pauline Frank. Teddy McKay. Rose Johnson. Sherry Charlie. Richard Johnson. Vicky Stewart.

And more than 50,000 other children.

1
October 11, 2009 – The Vatican

The unnoticed man stands before the oldest imperial Edifice in the world, and removes soil and water from his pocket. He is dressed simply, in vestments and regalia acquired over time. He shuts his eyes for a moment, and then begins to speak of children who are no more; and of those who are responsible.

Eventually, in front of the Edifice and in plain view of its security police and other Romans, the man will scatter the soil and its human remains and ask for the lies to vanish, and for something called 'justice'. He sprinkles sacred water on the ground. And he compels a false spirit to be banished from this place.

The man leaves, perhaps not entirely unnoticed now, for the next day, a tornado will rage through this place, the first one in decades; and in its wake, an official of the Edifice will ask to meet with him. Perhaps the dead will gain an audience now, too.

2
March 8, 1992 – Port Alberni, Canada

When I first drove into the Alberni valley on a cold spring morning, I noticed that the land was deep in shadow. It seemed to droop, weighed down by something more than the sporadic torrents of rain and the gray fog that crept up the inlet running snake-like from the Pacific Ocean.

Oddly, I felt an impulse to turn the car around and head back to the ferry to Vancouver. Over the valley, a spirit of genuine gloom seemed to hover, as palpable as flesh and bone.

I was heading for a job interview, hopeful of being hired as an ordained minister in this coastal town of 17,000 people. At the center of Vancouver Island, it had been the epicenter of a missionary invasion by my people extending back in time for more than a century. Now it was a dying lumber mill town, chopping up ever fewer of the majestic cedar trees that had once covered Vancouver Island.

Despite the decimation, the surrounding area was still nearly half populated by native Indians, and suffered from the highest poverty rate in the Province of British Columbia.

My destination, St Andrew's United Church in Port Alberni, was a dreary and sagging building on a tree-lined street in the north end of town. Nearby the church was the main road to the west coast, over which logging trucks bearing huge fallen grandfathers rumbled by every few minutes.

I was met at the front door by Fred Bishop, a short, wiry little guy. His voice cracked slightly as he introduced himself as the chairman of the church's Pastoral Relations Committee. He greeted me with a thin hard handful of knuckles.

'They're back here,' he said, with a slight nod. He seemed to find it difficult to crack a smile.

At the back of the church hall, ten polite faces greeted me from around a long wooden table as Fred ushered me into the room.

After the formalities of greeting, Fred Bishop asked me to say something about my background and the details of my personal life. I did so, especially concerning my extremely pregnant wife Anne, and my three-year-old daughter Clare.

My history, especially as a street worker in Toronto and on Vancouver's skid row, seemed to impress them. That, and perhaps my candor and openness even more. Within a very few minutes, I could tell that they wanted me, and were ready to hire me.

'We need new blood. There aren't many of us left,' commented an older woman, whose eyes and tired voice said it all. I'd seen the symptoms before.

Within the following week, Fred notified me that I'd been unanimously offered the job as their minister. I readily accepted.

I was by then thirty-six years old, and a happy husband and father – our second daughter Elinor made her appearance soon after the job interview, seemingly to cap my burst of good fortune. And so with my young family in tow, I settled in Port Alberni the following July. The somber, glowering weather I'd first encountered had given way to a typical bright west coast summer.

At first, I didn't take much notice of the native people in town. Most of them remained out of sight, or innocuous. I saw a few of them on the streets of the town during our first days there, but on my first Sunday in the pulpit at St Andrew's, I noticed that there was not a single native person to be seen in my church.

Instead, perhaps twenty aging white parishioners stared back at me expectantly on that first Sunday morning, looking to me, I supposed, to save their little flock, perhaps to restore what they thought their church should be.

After the service, as people milled around the coffee table, and as I struggled amid the banter to remember all their names, I sensed a tense avoidance in many of them, as if beneath the pleasant demeanor they harbored some family secret that they didn't want revealed.

Some of that apparent secret spilled out as I chatted with Fred Bishop, my straight-faced board chairman. In addition to his position as major-domo of St Andrew's, it seemed he was also a former mayor of the town and an executive with the local logging baron, MacMillan Bloedel. Fred's family, I learned right away because he lost no time in telling me, had been among the first Europeans to settle in the Alberni valley.

'They were pioneers here in the early 1860s, as a matter of fact,' said Fred. 'That was right about when a smallpox epidemic wiped out most of the Indians.'

That observation may have carried a slight pregnant undertone, as if to suggest a hidden message. Fred, I was soon to learn, knew all of the local history. As well as the secrets.

'Really,' I responded, not sure what to say. I watched him sip his tea, looking at me over the rim of the cup. I breathed deeply and said,

'Fred, I couldn't help but notice that there were no Indians in church today.'

Fred nearly choked on his tea. He coughed, clearing his throat, and set his cup down on the table.

'They keep to themselves pretty much as a general rule. And we keep to ourselves.' He glanced around the small gathering, then back to me. 'Everybody likes it that way.'

Noting his agitation, I didn't pursue the subject, but Fred's statement as well as his reaction haunted me all that first week.

I didn't know how to approach the aboriginal people, but as it turned out, it wasn't necessary, for they came to me. Within a few days of Fred's comment, I received a phone call from a man who introduced himself as Danny Gus. Danny was a retired native fisherman living west of town, on the Tseshaht Indian reservation, which was a stone's throw from the former Alberni Indian Residential School. I knew that my church had run that school for over fifty years but I knew nothing about the place. He welcomed me and lost no time in requesting a house call.

'I'd be glad to,' I said. 'What's the occasion, if I can ask?'

A chuckle at the other end of the line.

'Me an' Clothilda want to get married.'

'That's great,' I said. 'Congratulations.'

'Yeah. Our grandkids are coming along, an' we figure it's about time after forty years I make a honest woman out of 'er.'

We both laughed.

'Say, Reveren',' he continued. 'You suppose I need some marriage counselin' first?'

'Are you kidding?' I said. 'You guys could probably teach me something.'

The next day I drove out to Danny's place, and entered the reservation for the first time. He and Clothilda lived in a sagging and mossy shack a hundred feet from the former residential school grounds, which were now the location of the local tribal council office. Crouching above the dark Somass River, the old school ground that had swallowed up so many of Danny's people was shadowed and dripping with rain when I first saw it. Danny and Clothilda met me at the door, both heavy set and tired-looking people. We sat down in a cluttered living room adorned with pictures of family and friends.

With little ceremony, Clothilda brought mugs of tea to the table and then produced servings of chummis, which is salmon eggs in oil, and tastes as bad as it sounds. But I did the white liberal thing, pretending to like the stuff, and she kept loading me up with the greasy mixture.

I learned my lesson that day.

After a time, the conversation slackened, and Danny, sitting by the window, kept looking at the grounds of the former residential school.

Ignorant of any of its history, I said quickly,

'I've been wondering why there aren't any native people in my church. I know a lot of you are connected to the United Church...'

Danny turned and looked at me, and his eyes silenced me. He removed the pipe which he'd just lit from his mouth and stroked his temple with the stem. Then he shook his head, and looked out the window again. After a long moment of silence, he mumbled,

'They killed my best friend in that residential school of theirs. Beat him to death one night because he was crying so much. And then they buried him in the hill out back. The church people know it, and they don't want us in their church.'

3
August 27, 1996 – Vancouver, Canada

The austere, late middle-aged man leans forward to speak into a micro-phone.

'*For the record, my name is Dr Jon Jessiman. I've been asked to preside as judicial officer in this formal hearing conducted by the British Columbia Conference of the United Church of Canada. It concerns Reverend Kevin Annett and Comox-Nanaimo Presbytery's request that Reverend Annett's name be placed on the church's Discontinued Service List.*

'*Seated with me are the members of the Hearing Panel: Reverend Mollie Williams, as chairperson; Reverend Eleanor O'Neill, secretary; Geoffrey H. Wilkins, and Iain Benson, appearing for the applicant; and finally a qualified court reporter.*'
He pauses, and adds,

'*May the record show that it is 9:00 am, August 28, 1996 and that this is the meeting room of St John's United Church in Vancouver, British Columbia.*

'*Let me emphasize that this is not a court of law, but it will be operated according to the internal rules of a United Church disciplinary hearing. The purpose of the hearing is to determine whether the BC Conference should accept the recommendation made by the Presbytery, that Reverend Kevin Annett be delisted as an ordained minister. The hearing will operate at all times under the rules of evidence and due process of the province of British Columbia.*' *Dr Jessiman leans forward.* '*Is this clear, Mr Annett?*'
The accused leans forward slightly. He is seated in a wooden armchair

facing the table and Panel. In his dark suit and clerical collar, he appears to be of medium height; above his rimless glasses he has a high broad forehead and long retreating hair that curls over his ears and neck in the manner of a young Ben Franklin. He responds with a clear voice.

'I would like to ask of the Panel something I have been requesting for more than a year: the cause of my removal from my church by Presbytery, the charges against me, and the names of those who have accused me.

'Also, I'd like to ask the Panel to define what the grounds are for the delisting of a United Church minister. All of this information is needed if I am to be allowed to prepare my defense.'

He addresses Dr Jessiman, but it is Mollie Williams, as chairperson of the Panel, who appears agitated, and turns to huddle with Jessiman, speaking behind one raised hand. After a moment she nods and turns to face Kevin Annett.

'Reverend Annett, there are no charges against you. This hearing is called in response to a recommendation by Comox-Nanaimo Presbytery that your name be removed from the Active Service List of Ministers. There are no stated criteria for delisting a minister. Those will be determined by the Panel at the end of this hearing.'

Rather than shock, there is something akin to a sad familiarity in his eyes as he responds,

'If there are no charges against me, and I can't know what the criteria are by which you're judging me, then how can I conduct any kind of defense?' *The judicial officer, Jon Jessiman, replies that this request is out of order and not relevant to the proceedings.*

'May I ask,' *says Reverend Annett,* 'how a request for due process can be "out of order"?'

There is no answer from Dr Jessiman. Instead, turning slightly to his left, he says,

'Prior to proceeding with this case, the Panel should be aware of the *facts of this case. Mr Benson?'*

Iain Benson, a small, angry-looking man, rises from his seat next to Dr Jessiman. Benson is a Catholic lawyer hired by the Presbytery to undertake Kevin Annett's expulsion as a clergyman.

'Mr Annett,' Benson reads from a single sheet of paper, 'is a forty-year-old minister of the United Church who graduated from Vancouver School of Theology in 1990 with the degree of Master of Divinity, and was ordained by the Church in May of that year. He had previously received a Bachelor's degree in anthropology and a Master's degree in political science from the same university. In 1992, he sought a vacant position at the St Andrew's United pastoral charge in Port Alberni and was hired there in July of that year.

'Mr Annett's ministry came to an end at St Andrew's in January 1995, some two and one half years after his arrival in Port Alberni, because he failed to maintain the peace and welfare of the church.'

The only thing he left out, Kevin Annett says to himself, is my time in law school.

'Mr Benson,' says the chairperson, 'would you call your first witness?'

Iain Benson moves to a position facing the long table. 'As the first of four witnesses, I call Bob Stiven, who was the chairman of Comox-Nanaimo Presbytery at the time of Reverend Annett's removal from his position at St Andrew's Church in Port Alberni.'

4
1992–1993 – Port Alberni, Canada

By all indicators, my family and I had moved to one of the worst places in the province.

The year I arrived in Port Alberni, a survey by the provincial government revealed that the town had the worst rate of family violence and child poverty in British Columbia – although few of my parishioners wanted to talk about it. Every day, I observed that reality walking the streets of Port Alberni, and encountered it in the lives that began entering mine. Some of it even began to enter our comfortable little church, especially when I opened the doors and launched a food bank in our church basement.

We called the effort 'Loaves and Fishes' after the name was suggested by a feisty native woman named Debbie Seward who had begun to frequent my church together with her family and friends.

A month after I began at St Andrew's, another native woman named Karen Connerley walked into St Andrew's on a Sunday morning, accompanied by her two children, Eric and Kendra. Indian-style, Karen let her kids run free as she took her seat. One of the women in the congregation asked Karen to leave.

'Fuck you, bitch!' Karen replied precisely if not subtly. The red-faced church lady glared at me before storming from the church.

The white lady was to return, eventually, and actually became one of my strongest supporters. She came to know Karen and her kids as well, often driving them to church or to our food bank. But it took that first confrontation for the unspoken to be said, like a key opening an encrusted and forbidden door.

More was said, by Karen and her kids, that first Sunday.

I was preaching that morning about the Good Samaritan,

about the dangerous necessity of stopping to help a suffering stranger, especially someone we had been taught to fear. At one point in my homily, Karen spoke up and interrupted me, to the turned heads of the congregation:

'That's like what us Indians face, you know, Reverend.'

No one said anything, until I replied,

'No, I don't know. Tell me.'

Karen looked about, suddenly nervous, but she continued.

'Kendra here gets sick all the time. The doctors don't do nothin'. I wanted to bring her here so she wouldn't end up like Charlie junior.'

One of the ushers at the back of the church stood up suddenly and strode out of the church, slamming the door behind him. Nervous pale faces swiveled to me, thir eyes pleading or raging at me to deal with this threatening intruder. But all I could see were Karen's own desperate brown eyes.

'What happened to Charlie?' I asked her.

'He was my first born. He died of pneumonia last year, that's what they called it. We took him to the hospital but they wouldn't help him. Nobody would. I was thinking of him when you were talking, because it's too bad that good man in the story wasn't here to help Charlie.'

One of the white women began to cry and some of the angry eyes softened.

I was about to say something, but I realized that there was no need. Karen had summed up the message better than I could.

Kendra and her brother grabbed most of the cookies during the coffee hour afterward, while their reddened and runny eyes and grasping hands spoke volumes about aboriginal life in Port Alberni. And so the door that would eventually lead to more than illness and neglect began to open.

A woman called Virginia nudged it open even further a few weeks later. I couldn't pronounce her Indian name, so I called her by her Caucasian one. She approached me after the church service, a cup of coffee in one hand, with what I thought was an oddly flirtatious look.

Sure enough, she said to me,

'I'm Virginia but you can call me Virgin for short.'

One eyebrow arched slightly; she seemed somehow both amused and aggrieved. Perhaps it was whimsical, her accosting a white guy, attempting to explain something to him, of all people.

'I heard what you said today,' she continued, in a quieter tone. 'You know, at this residential school, the principal rewarded the boys when they memorized the Ten Commandments,' she added, her eyes on me as if awaiting my reaction.

'Uh-huh?' I said a little impatiently, as people milled all about us.

'One after another. In his bedroom.'

Seeing my frowning ignorance, she continued,

'If they could recite all Ten Commandments, he ass-fucked them. That was their reward.'

I shook my head with moral outrage, and said,

'Whatever happened to that guy?'

Virginia laughed for the first time.

'Oh, he was in charge of the Alberni school for a long time. He was the one who used the electric cattle prod on my brother. He retired from there.'

'And the police were never told?' I protested.

Virginia kept her eyes leveled on me.

'You've got a lot to learn, Kevin,' was all she said.

My education began early in Port Alberni. And it escalated rapidly. It was not so much that I set out to dig too deeply into the lives of the native people who began coming to my church. But the more I became acquainted with the local aboriginals, the more I was struck with how deeply the roots of their suffering went, and how little I knew about those roots. To know them, I discovered, I had to forget most of what I had been taught, especially about the history of Canada and my own church.

One of my first rude awakenings came with the number of funerals I had to conduct on the local Indian reservations. Many of them were for teenagers who had killed themselves, or for infant children.

I remembered, long before, reading newspaper accounts of the sheer frequency of Indian suicide cases. Usually, they were described with consternation by reporters and astonished social workers alike, especially the cases among younger aboriginals.

'Why are so many young Indians killing themselves?' asked those media commentators who took the time to care. But now I was being confronted with the answer, up close and personal. For as I drew nearer to native families, and spent long hours listening to their stories without trying to recruit them to join my church, men and women began to speak to me about why it was that so much of the suicides and suffering among them stemmed from the Indian residential schools.

I knew very little about the schools, except for the version that the church had divulged to me when I had inquired.

'Those schools were our pride and joy,' said Oliver Howard, my predecessor at St Andrew's and a former coastal missionary who helped 'orient' me to the area.

'It was our mission, our program, to raise up a dying race, to bring them the Good News.'

On the contrary, what I was beginning to learn from the survivors and their families was that it had all been very bad news.

I learned, first by word of mouth and later as I began to investigate for myself, how the Royal Canadian Mounted Police and clergymen had appeared in native villages and grabbed infants as young as three out of the arms of parents who were beaten to the ground if they resisted.

Faced with jail if they wouldn't comply, aboriginal parents were forced by a federal law to sign releases called 'Application for Admission' forms which surrendered legal guardianship over their own children to the principals and their sponsoring churches. Their children were taken away, many never to be seen again. I was to learn later that nearly half of them died in the schools from deliberate disease, malnutrition, outright homicide, and often, a broken heart.

Some of this tragedy I began to learn about during the week, when my eldest daughter Clare and I often drove out to the local reserves and delivered bread and other freebies to the children there. I can see with a clarity sharpened by time how my blue-eyed four-year-old would stare incredulously at the hordes of native children who ran from all directions to seize the bread with joy and laughter. After a few visits, Clare cautiously offered me her gummy bear candies and said that the kids could have those, too.

That first year before Christmas – always a bad time for suicides – I was called out to one of these same reserves, the Tseshaht reservation west of town, to preside at yet another funeral. This time it happened to be for a baby who had died suddenly. I had been in town barely six months, but many of the local natives already knew about me. The family all met me on the front lawn, and the grandfather, Richard, as part of the funeral service, asked me to baptize each member of his family.

'We all need protection,' he said.

'Protection from what?' I asked.

I thought at first that he was feeling insulted at the directness of my words, but then Richard took me by the arm, led me to one side, and said quietly,

'The soul of this child won't rest and will come back and claim one of us.'

I nodded, but far from understanding, I said, 'Why won't he rest?'

Richard looked at me carefully, as if hesitating to take me into his confidence. Quietly, slowly, he replied,

'He's with all the other children who died here. None of them can rest.'I remembered Danny Gus then, and his mentioning of his friend who had been killed. I said,

'Richard, do you mean the kids who died up at the residential school?'

Richard appeared to relax, relieved that I knew. He nodded. A sudden light came into his eyes.

'I'm glad you came here today' he said, taking my hand.

I worried a little how my church board would react if they knew that I had baptized more than a dozen non-church members at their home that day – and Indians at that. But none of that seemed to matter to me, as I conducted the rite. Suddenly I was part of a mystery I couldn't understand, but which I knew I had to uncover. After the ceremony we all ate together, as was their custom. Around a small living room we chewed at salmon and bannock, and people began to talk about the local residential school, for they seemed to feel safe now.

I left their home hours later, dazed and raw. I couldn't believe the stories I had heard.

'They're just making that stuff up,' declared my wife, Anne McNamee, when I shared with her some of what I'd heard that evening.

She wasn't alone in her thinking. I kept speaking about what I was learning, confiding in the people to whom I thought I could turn, my colleagues in the United Church. Their reaction was universally the same as Anne's, except angrier and in greater denial.

'They hate us for taking their land, so they'll say anything bad about us,' declared a former classmate of mine from seminary named Foster Freed, who would eventually help have me fired. He ministered to an affluent white church in Parksville, farther east on Vancouver Island.

'I mean, do you really think we went around murdering children?'

His words haunted me and tempted me to doubt what I had

learned. Were my own people capable of mass murder? Here and now, in this century, in this place?

History, of course, saw nothing wrong with such a proposition. Like many, I knew the brutal facts of North American history – and the record of torture, mass murder and Inquisition that are synonymous with European Christianity.

But those nightmarish events seemed utterly distant and remote from the United Church of Canada, in which I had been raised. I thought of the happy Sunday school, the church outings, the chicken suppers, the CARE packages we sent to Haiti, and the endless sermons talking of justice in the world and of the love of Jesus.

And yet, the local native people had told me of seeing children being strapped into a homemade electric chair in the United Church's Alberni residential school basement, and how they jumped and even died from the electric shocks; of nails and needles rammed through the tongues of five-year-olds for speaking in their own language; of little girls raped by clergymen and then murdered to hide the evidence of their pregnancy; of children lined up as if in a slave auction and carted off by 'visiting dignitaries', never to be seen again.

Talk of two solitudes! Which reality was true? Or were they both?

Back then, there was only one way I thought I could be sure: by learning more from the actual eyewitnesses, and giving their voices a chance to be heard. I had no reason not to believe what I thought was the obvious: if the church really knew the truth about what had gone on, it would not only own up to its sordid history but would bring to justice those responsible. And so, in the early days of 1993, I began to open my pulpit to the congregation as a kind of collective sermon, believing that if the voice of the people really is the voice of God, then no one would fear that voice.

5
August 28, 1996 – Vancouver, Canada

*Then shall [God] say also unto them [who are condemned], 'Depart
from me, ye cursed, into everlasting fire, prepared for the devil and
his angels.'*
Matthew 25:41, AV

*Iain Benson is not a doctor either of jurisprudence or divinity, but a
lawyer, and one who is known to have pocketed well over $60,000 from
the United Church for his efforts to discredit and defrock Reverend
Kevin Annett. But his voice quavers in an unlawyerly manner as he
stands in front of the Panel.*
'I call Reverend Bob Stiven.'
Stiven takes a seat and is sworn. He is short, wiry-haired and red-faced.

*Looking up from his notes, Iain Benson asks: 'What is your position,
Bob?'*
'I'm President of the Presbytery. Comox-Nanaimo Presbytery.'
*Kevin Annett stares at the man. He has met him once or twice before
now, but Stiven has never attended St Andrew's Church or seen Kevin
Annett in action.*

*'For the record,' says Benson, 'Mr Stiven is being called as an expert
witness concerning Reverend Annett. Now, Bob, what can you please
tell us about Kevin Annett's effectiveness as a minister?'*
*'Not much. It's not that we, uh, I never was there on a Sunday, if that's
what you mean. But I know that he was paying too little attention to
the gray-haired English grannies who are the backbone of our church.'*
*The Panel hearing is filled with observers, at least two dozen witnesses
who have been invited to watch the proceedings. Several of them erupt*

with laughter at Stiven's comment.

'You can laugh if you like,' says Stiven, 'but there's no way Kevin had a future in our Presbytery, not with all that social justice stuff he was preaching.'
The room falls silent. Dr Jessiman seems for a moment to be experiencing cardiac arrest. He gets to his feet and lumbers to where Iain Benson is standing beside the witness chair. He says something to Benson behind his raised notes, and then returns to the long table.

Benson clears his throat.

'But Bob, wouldn't you say that Reverend Annett received fair treatment in the courts of our church?'

Bob Stiven looks around, seemingly confused.

'Look, in my rage, there's no way Kevin would have received a fair hearing in my Presbytery – not after he started soundin' off about all those dead Indian kids.'
Kevin Annett has trouble restraining himself from performing a victory dance. Has this grim official not just destroyed the church's whole credibility and case, by literally admitting the Presbytery's hostility to 'Indian-lovers'?

Dr Jessiman resumes control.

'Mr Benson, it's close to lunch time. I'm going to suggest we recess for an hour.'
Without informing Kevin Annett, Jessiman, Benson, the entire Panel and even the court reporter then have lunch together at a nearby expensive restaurant, on the church's tab, of course – a practice continued by all of them over the following seven months of the hearing.

Reconvening later, Dr Jessiman turns to his lunch partners.

'Members of the Panel, I'm going to instruct you to disregard Bob Stiven's previous testimony on the grounds that it is not relevant to the issue of Reverend Annett's suitability for ministry.'
Kevin Annett stands quickly.

'Dr Jessiman, how can a Presbytery member's opinion of me not be relevant, since the whole issue here is Presbytery's position on my suitability for ministry?'
'I find your remarks disruptive, Mr Annett, and I question your motives.'

Kevin Annett jots down that Dr Jessiman is not only both prosecutor and judge, but is bolstering weak evidence by attacking the witness: a technique Annett recalls being taught in a 'Legal Process' course at the University of BC's law school more than a decade earlier. 'Madam Chairperson,' *says Kevin Annett,* 'Mr Stiven by his own admission has only spoken to me on two occasions before this hearing and that over a period of three years, entirely at Presbytery meetings. So his statements are pure hearsay, which has been disallowed by your own rules of evidence.' 'That is irrelevant,' *says Reverend Williams.* 'Proceed, Mr Benson.'
Iain Benson is smirking behind an uplifted hand.

'So, Bob, how would you describe Kevin Annett's suitability for ministry?'
The wiry official is beginning to perspire. 'All I know is a lot of people in the pews were upset with the changes Kevin was introducing so fast.' 'How did you know that?' 'People talk, you know. I just heard things.' *Kevin Annett rises again.* 'Dr Jessiman, is such a hearsay statement allowed to stand?' 'The statement is not hearsay,' *comments Jessiman.*
'Excuse me?' *Kevin replies.*

'The Panel concurs with Dr Jessiman,' comments Panel chair Williams. 'Why am I not surprised?' says Kevin Annett. 'Your delisting hearing is intentionally not following its own "Rules of Evidence or Procedure".' There is no response, until Dr Jessiman says: 'Reverend Annett, you may cross-examine the witness if you wish.'

Iain Benson glances with seeming surprise at Jessiman, but meekly takes his seat.

Kevin Annett stands before Bob Stiven, who turns away from him nervously, frowning.

'Bob, did you have any first-hand experience of my ministry in Port Alberni?''I heard reports from people. I saw the effect you were having.''But what first-hand experience?'

'I didn't need to see for myself when people were telling me how you were upsetting them and causing such conflict.''What people?'Stiven remains silent.

'Mr Stiven, did you know that my congregation had a long history of discord and factionalism, of fighting among themselves and with their ministers, long before I ever arrived?''I'm not aware of that, no.''Well, you must have been, since a conflict resolution mediator from the Vancouver School of Theology met with my congregation in the fall of 1993 and issued a report to that effect to me and your Presbytery. Did you never see a copy of her report?'Stiven remains silent.

'Did you know that three of the previous four ministers who preceded me at St Andrew's had been forced from their pulpit by factions in the congregation?'Stiven remains silent.

'Can you tell me then why I was scapegoated and blamed by your Presbytery for this conflict when it originated before I got there? And why I was removed from my pulpit on a false pretext?'Stiven remains silent.

Kevin Annett turns to the Panel table.

'May I request that Mr Stiven answer my last question?''I'm going to

intervene,' says Dr Jessiman. 'I rule that Mr Stiven's testimony is now concluded.''Pardon me?' says Kevin.
'And I suggest that the Panel adjourn for the day.'

6
Interlude – Let Us Prey

Punish [your child] with the rod,
and save his soul from death.
Proverbs 23:14, New International Version

Reverend Russell Crossley raped women and even young girls for over thirty years before he was arrested. The truth is he was caught right away, in the mid 1960s, when as a young clergyman in the United Church he was named as a rapist by one of the parishioners whom he had assaulted.

The church lawyers gathered and convinced the victim not to press charges against Crossley. Then they had him moved to another unsuspecting parish in Ontario, where he started raping all over again.

That went on for decades. Each time, after the latest rape, someone would come forward and spill the beans, and she would be silenced and Crossley would be shielded by the church and quietly shuffled to another group of innocent lambs. The rapes and cover up went on, and on.

The rapist was nearing retirement years when his past finally caught him, thanks to the persistence of one of his victims, who wouldn't be silenced. She pressed charges, along with others Crossley had assaulted, including an (at the time) underage minor. The Royal Canadian Mounted Police (RCMP) threatened and cajoled these latest victims, but they wouldn't stop. And so reluctantly, in the spring of 1998, the cops arrested Crossley and he faced trial in Victoria, BC, where he had enjoyed a 'prospering ministry' at Metropolitan United Church.

His trial revealed the kind of friends he had, including former United Church moderators, RCMP superintendents, and other prominent men who stepped forward to give character references for the rapist. Church people poured out their empathy for Crossley, not for those innocents he had violated. And so, dutifully, the judge slapped his wrist with a six-month prison term, most of which he didn't serve.

After he walked free from prison, Russell Crossley resumed his ministry; indeed, he had remained on salary with the church even after having been convicted of rape and assault. Elated, his congregation and the BC Conference of the United Church lauded him with testimonial dinners and awards for 'thirty-five years of successful ministry'. And Crossley continued in the pulpit until the fall of 2008, when he finally retired, on full pension.

By way of a contrast:

- During exactly the same time, and in the same church body where Russell Crossley was being exonerated for his crime, Kevin Annett faced ostracism, persecution, expulsion and professional ruination for having named some of the United Church's dirty secrets involving stolen native land and murdered Indian children

- Kevin Annett too was a United Church minister, although with none of the institutional pull exercised by Crossley. He had never sat on the church's national governing body or written the church's books and faith statement documents, as had Russell Crossley. Nor did he number as his friends RCMP commissioners or politicians.

- Kevin Annett is not a rapist, as is Russell Crossley. But today he remains an officially defrocked United Church minister and Crossley is not.

- Kevin Annett faces daily slandering and defamation from the church and its allies, and Russell Crossley does not.

- Kevin Annett is still a 'man to be avoided' by respectable church society, and Russell Crossley is officially admired and honored.

A cynical or perhaps clear-sighted person might conclude that it pays to do the wrong thing, not the right, in the church of Jesus Christ – or at least, in the United Church of Canada.

Perhaps Kevin Annett's main mistake was not knowing of what he was a part. Nothing that his Sunday school teacher or seminary instructors taught him prepared him for the fact that rape, murder and most other beastly crimes go on with impunity in the Christian churches, and even in the all-Canadian, liberal-seeming United Church, and that these crimes appear to be valued, and certainly go unpunished.

Yet experience is a cruel teacher, and Kevin Annett certainly received enough clues along the way about the actual nature of official Christianity, one of the most memorable being when a United Church lawyer named Paul Mills, when told by Kevin of drug dealing and prostitution going on in the Toronto Fred Victor Mission where he worked, said simply,

'I know about all that. The only problem here is that you wrote a letter about it.'

Perhaps the real problem all goes back to Genesis and the odd Christian notion of 'fallen innocence', of how there is something suspect in anything that is good, untouched, and seemingly unblemished. There can't be any such thing, after all, in a 'cursed' world like ours. And so wherever it manifests itself, innocence is a mockery to Christianity's entire faith and worldview, whether that's the untouched splendor of an unlogged rainforest, or the unalloyed integrity of one man, or the happy cries of a child who is different from us. And so that purity must be crushed.

God did exactly that, after all, to his own Son Jesus – according to the church's Bible, the most pure and perfect being ever created. This radiant being was offered up, tortured and killed by his own Dad. The fact that the obligatory justification of all abusers, that something good came out of the crime, is tacked onto the biblical story as a sort of redemption for the rest of us, doesn't detract from the basic message: don't be good and innocent – it will get you nailed.

So is it surprising at all that a clergyman can rape and violate at will for decades, and be encouraged in his crime by the Christian church and its top leaders? Or, that another clergyman can be destroyed and sacrificed publicly by the same leaders for simply asking why such things can happen?

7
March 1993 – Port Alberni, Canada

God is granting to our Empire mastery of the world for having brought the light of His word to the dark regions of mankind.
World Conference of Protestant Missionaries, London, 1888

On the first Sunday morning that I announced an open pulpit in my church, Alfred Keitlah, a traditional chief of the Ahousaht aboriginal people, stood up and spoke in his own language, offering a prayer of thanksgiving for all of us there.

The congregation had more than doubled in just over six months, and aboriginals and poor white people had begun coming regularly to my church. But opening the pulpit didn't happen easily, at first. On this occasion, I had simply announced that anyone was free to comment on what I had preached about, or whatever they might have on their mind. Then I sat down and waited.

Nothing happened for several minutes, as people coughed nervously or rustled their bulletins. Then an elderly aboriginal man named Alfred Keitlah took me at my word.

Alfred was hardly an impressive figure, frail in stature, and shaking. Yet as his voice reverberated in that sanctuary, it seemed to me that he was reclaiming a space that had been taken away long ago. For here, on this very ground where St Andrew's stood, the first Presbyterian mission had been built more than a century earlier, from whence the attempted extermination of Alfred's people had been launched.

A different sort of door was opened that morning, and I realized that from then on, everyone in church would in some fashion be compelled to make a choice, although not necessarily the obvious one, between whether or not to let the Indians in, or keep them out.

Rather, it would be the choice – which I tried to address in sermons, Bible study classes and during my discussions with people – of whether ours would be a congregation that took Jesus' words seriously, and actually tried to build a community of equality and justice.

Easier said than done, of course. Much easier.

The native people coming to my church seemed unable to imagine 'justice' without addressing what had happened to them, especially in the residential school. And the last thing most of the white parishioners wanted to hear about was what their church had done to the very native people who began to sit next to them on Sundays. People began to collide. One Sunday morning not long after Alfred Keitlah had broken the ice, an older Ahousaht woman named Florence tried to speak from the pulpit about how she had been raped by a clergyman at the local residential school. As she haltingly described what had happened, a white woman, one of the 'old guard' of the church, stood and yelled out:

'I won't have the reputation of good Christians besmirched any more from this pulpit!'

She then stormed out of the church, followed by her immediate family.

The incensed woman, as it turned out, was the daughter of the man who had raped the Ahousaht woman when she'd been a child. That would later be verified with names, dates and details, including reports of a subsequent murder, but for now the mystery was still conjecture. And violently opposed.

But now, embarrassed, Florence sat down quickly, and several natives hurried from the church. A line had been crossed, and everybody knew it.

Not surprisingly, Fred Bishop approached me later that day for one of those avuncular 'chats' that precede any institutional retaliation against wayward elements, the likes of which I was undoubtedly becoming in the eyes of Fred and his crowd. It was after church, during coffee hour, and as my eldest child Clare and other kids were careening around the church auditorium, and I was making my usual attempt to listen to several people at the same time, Fred approached me like the former mayor he was, and demanded a moment of my time. 'This can't wait,' he declared shakily.

Inside the church office, Fred didn't bother to sit down, but laid down the law without delay. I had little doubt that Fred was under pressure from somewhere.

'The congregation is getting concerned about the direction you're taking them,' he said matter-of-factly.

'The congregation?' I replied, confused. 'You mean, everyone?'

Red-faced, he answered, 'The ones who matter. The people who have held this church together for years. They're getting fed up with so many, uh, newcomers in the pews. Worship service is turning into a circus, Kevin.'

'By newcomers, do you mean Indians?'

Fred sighed and shook his head.

'That's not the issue. Your sermons are mostly on social justice and the poor. You don't preach enough about biblical themes.'

'The poor *are* mentioned over 1,200 times in the Bible, Fred.'

'Listen, you're causing division in our church. You spend more time visiting these, uh, non-members, than you do seeing the congregation.'

'That's just not true. I spend most of my week doing pastoral visits with everyone; you know that. Besides, the ones you call 'non-members' go to this church, too. I consider all of them my parish.'

The older man threw up both hands and shook his head.

'Look, Kevin, if you don't stop all this social work and just start being a minister, I can't be responsible for what might happen to you.' He let that one sink in for a moment, then swung around abruptly and left the office.

Fred's dire warning hung like a pall over me after that. The period that followed was strangely contradictory: on the one hand it was a time of great satisfaction and happiness, as my daughters grew and changed, and I basked each day in our love, and as that same love caused our work to spill over from the pews of my church into the wider community. Yet on the other hand, darkly overshadowing all of this, was a growing sense that I was living with a Damoclean warning not to look too deeply beneath the surface of things.

Meanwhile, I was in constant demand, working over seventy hours each week; and in my daily round of counseling, funerals, and endless visits, I came to know hundreds of people intimately.

I received a shower of small but real affirmations from them, in addition to the long hugs and often tearful expressions of gratitude each Sunday. One evening a small salmon was left on our back porch. But a week later, a seagull was left on the hood of my car, garroted, the cord still circling its neck.

That chilling sequel to a gesture of love brought home forcibly the dichotomy of my situation: this strange mixture of love and death in the valley.

But another shoe was about to drop. It happened a short time later, at the spring meeting of our local Presbytery, a normally banal confluence of United Church ministers.

Amidst the mundane routine of the Presbytery meeting, my predecessor at St Andrew's, the crusty retired minister named Oliver Howard who had first spoken to me about his pride in the local residential school, rose to present an official report on a century of our United Church's work with the Ahousaht people.

'It's a long and proud history,' said old Oliver with a sort of grumpy evangelism, 'and the Indians' appreciation of the coming of Christianity is plain to see. They've expressed it to me many times.'

Nobody said anything at that point, as the old guy looked around the room. But his pedestrian approach suddenly changed gears when he exclaimed,

'All this talk of land claims and sovereignty by the Indians doesn't mean anything if they aren't willing to come into the twentieth century and integrate into our culture. That's what we've been trying to show them all these years. Especially out in Ahousaht.'

A shock seemed to ripple through the crowd as the word 'Ahousaht' was mentioned. People began to buzz, and frown.

I had heard about the Ahousahts of course, especially through Albert Keitlah and other natives who had spoken in my church. I often went to the Ahousaht village on the west coast to officiate at funerals and weddings, and some of their people were attending my church.

I felt I had to say something, especially in response to Oliver's warmed-over racism. So after he sat down, I arose and said,

'I'd like to suggest we hold our next presbytery meeting in Ahousaht, so we can hear from the people there themselves.'

A bomb might just as well have gone off. Three delegates actually leaped up at the same time, trying to speak over each other.

'They don't want us there,' one old guy blustered. 'They don't want anything to do with us!'

Another speaker was saying something about how the Ahousahts were all 'dysfunctional'.

'Wait and see,' one woman hissed at me. 'In a few years they'll own the whole province.'

Needless to say, there was no further mention of my suggestion, and the meeting broke up shortly thereafter. But I was accosted later that afternoon by an affable guy named Bill Howie – a senior church official, given to back-clapping and broad smiles, who would later figure in my firing.

'Kevin!' he said. 'I've been meaning to have a word with you, since this is your first meeting with us.'

Howie looked around the gathering and then at me with his steel-gray eyes, the smile still broad. 'You have a promising future with the church. And of course a young family to provide for.' Again the flashy smile. 'So be careful. Don't believe everything you hear about the native people here. Especially when it comes to the Ahousahts.'

Shortly after, as I struggled to make sense of Howie's veiled threat, I was approached by Bruce Gunn, a fellow clergyman who ministered among the Ahousahts on Flores Island out on the Pacific coast.

'You sure raised the temperature here,' he said.

'What's this thing about the Ahousahts? There seems to be a lot of fear about them.'

Bruce nodded and smiled.

'Why don't you come up to Ahousaht next Thursday and see for yourself? There's someone I want you to meet.'

8
June 13, 1998 – Vancouver, Canada

We bestow suitable favors and special graces on those Catholic kings and princes, athletes and intrepid champions of the Christian faith ... to invade, search out, capture, vanquish, and subdue all Saracens and pagans whatsoever, and other enemies of Christ wheresoever placed, and to reduce their persons to perpetual slavery, and to apply and appropriate possessions, and goods, and to convert them to their use and profit.

Papal Bull *Romanus Pontifex*, January 8, 1455, Rome

Transcript from the Northwest Tribunal into Canadian Indian Residential Schools, sponsored by the United Nations affiliate IHRAAM – 10:31 am

Tribunal Judge Royce White Calf: Now can I ask you Mr Sylvester, what was done to you by the doctors at the Kuper Island residential school?

Witness Arnold Sylvester: It's been fifty years but I'll never forget ... I was, there was a group of us, fifty boys, we were all around ten, maybe eleven. The priest came and took us up to the infirmary there one morning, and that's where the German doctors gave us the shots.

Judge Royce White Calf: What shots? And they were Germans?

Witness Arnold Sylvester: Yes sir, they couldn't speak English at all. They had these guys to, you know, interpret for them. They gave us these shots, made us all really really sick. We threw up, was sick for days. A bunch of the boys died from it. Their bodies swelled up and they looked like balloons. Two shots, right near each nipple. And the whole time these Germans kept watching us, walking around our beds and taking notes.

Judge Royce White Calf: What were the names of some of these boys who died?

Witness Arnold Sylvester: I remember my friend Sandy Mitchell. He was from our village. He died from the shot. They told his family it was pneumonia. They took his body away and I never saw him again.

Judge Royce White Calf: Did anyone tell you what the shots were for, Arnold?

Witness Arnold Sylvester: No sir, they just said it was a test we had to do. But I can tell you why we got them. (pause) They wanted what we were sitting on. The land. The gold. The timber. And they got it.

9
April 1993 – Marktosis Village, Flores Island

The following week, I took Bruce Gunn up on his invitation to come to the Ahousaht community. I didn't know what to expect as I drove up the snake-like road toward the west coast of Vancouver Island.

The Ahousaht people live on Flores Island, a half-hour boat ride through the stormy, ocean-fed straits of the Clayoquot Sound. They had lived there for thousands of years, fishing, whaling and occasionally warring with other tribes such as the Ohiats and the Ucluelets. Their present population was a few hundred – all that remained from a population of more than 10,000 people who had held a much larger area before the white men arrived with their 'Good News' and smallpox.

As I drove west, I thought about Archbishop Desmond Tutu's comment on the history of South African colonial settlement: 'When the Europeans arrived, they had the Bible and we had the land. Now we have the Bible and they have the land.' As I was to learn, the United Church of Canada and its Presbyterian prede-cessors had acquired prime forested land all over the west coast for many decades, thanks to its partnership with Empire. Through a system known as 'Clergy Reserves', the English 'Crown', which arbitrarily claimed total ownership of all native land, allotted it to missionary churches, primarily the Roman Catholic, the Anglican, and the United Church. These churches made lots of money over the years selling off this stolen native land to corporate benefactors, notably large forestry companies – a practice that had been kept completely secret.

I was to learn all this and more not through official church channels, but from my friendship with Bruce and Ahousaht elders, in the days and weeks that followed this first visit by me to his pastoral charge on the Ahousaht reservation.

Bruce met me when I arrived at the ferry dock on Flores Island, next to the main village there, known as Marktosis. With him was a frail-appearing native woman, who looked right into my eyes as Bruce introduced us. If I felt awkward, she didn't make it any easier for me.

'If you are a friend of Bruce's, you are welcome,' she said without smiling. Then she added, 'But we don't like United Church ministers here much. They never stay long. Just long enough to steal something.'

Bruce grinned at me. The two of them accompanied me up what appeared to be the principal street of the town, not really a street, but a collection of sagging houses, cars without wheels and mountains of garbage parked among three-foot weeds, around which scampered a variety of dogs and screaming kids.

At the end of this slum row rose a wooden building, unpainted and dilapidated, surmounted by a cross. Bruce opened the front door. 'I share this with the local Catholic priest.'

'How ecumenical,' I said.

In a room at the back of the building, which I supposed served as Bruce's office, squatted a small desk, a couple of chairs and a bookcase. A naked light bulb was suspended from the ceiling. A gray-haired, older native man sat in one chair sipping from a cup.

'Kevin Annett, this is Chief Earl Maquinna George. He's the traditional elder here.'

We spoke for most of that day, as a sudden coastal squall blew up and hammered the building. The storm's arrival was matched by the shock of what I learned that afternoon. By evening, my view of my church was changed forever.

Not a mile from where we sat, according to Chief George, a parcel of hundreds of acres of land on the Ahousaht reservation known as Lot 363 had been basically stolen by Presbyterian (and later United Church) missionary John Ross in the early 1900s, and decades later sold off by Ross' grandson to MacMillan Bloedel, a corporation, popularly known as MacBlo, which was the largest forestry company in British Columbia. The land was now hungered after by the giant Weyerhaeuser Company of Seattle, the largest logging outfit in the world, whose corporate jaws had become set on the acquisition of its Canadian cousin MacBlo.

The smaller Canadian behemoth squatted like some feudal landlord over the land, forests and most of the people of the Alberni valley, including, as I was discovering, my employer, the United Church of Canada, which it regularly endowed with charitable donations.

So, like a distorted big-fish-little-fish cartoon, the church was the holder of stolen native land, MacMillan Bloedel wanted the rest of the trees on that land, and Weyerhaeuser wanted MacBlo. And lounging in the background like a *cosa nostra* Don was the Provincial NDP (New Democratic Party) government. A hybrid Canadian politique, the NDP embraced a sort of tepid socialism, laced with a ubiquitous yearning for a piece of the action.

Standing in the path of all these sequential machinations, in the best Cochise tradition, was the aging figure of the man with whom I now sat, Ahousaht hereditary Chief Earl Maquinna George.

As hereditary Keeper of the Land for the Ahousahts, Chief George's primary duty under their ancient tribal law was to protect the land given them by their Creator – and that included the land called Lot 363 by the pale men in suits who sat in church, corporate and governmental boardrooms.

In November of 1992, a short time after my arrival in Port Alberni, Chief Earl Maquinna George had written to the government of British Columbia. He declared that he was claiming all of Lot 363 for his people, and demanded that all the logging plans for that land be halted immediately.

All of this and what followed was painstakingly related to me by Bruce and Chief George, as we sat for hours in that rickety and rained-upon office, drinking endless cups of tea.

Bruce continued to explain that Chief George had the government, the companies involved and the United Church behind the eight-ball, since the province was at precisely that time in the throes of extensive land claims and treaty negotiations. So Chief George's demand could not be ignored, and a halt was ordered on all tree cutting on Lot 363.

One can only imagine the howls of rage and frustration in the boardrooms in Vancouver and Seattle and, by extension, the more 'saintly' enclave of the United Church in Toronto.

The provincial government in Victoria and the United Church were both suddenly on the hot seat, because Chief George was also insisting that all of the original owners of the land be included in the Lot 363 negotiations.

'That of course would have included the United Church,' said Bruce, refilling my mug, 'because their original missionary had hustled the Ahousahts out of that parcel of land as early as 1904.'

The United Church was about to be publicly exposed as profiteers in stolen aboriginal land. To make it that more interesting, Lot 363 had also housed the church's Ahousaht Indian Residential School, which was shortly to come under scrutiny for a history of crimes, including alleged murders. In short, these revelations threatened to do the church irreparable damage, as murder will and does come out.

For government, church and corporate agendas, the timing couldn't have been worse. The previous year, the largest sustained protest in British Columbia history had taken place just a few miles from St Andrew's Church, in the Clayoquot Sound basin, when thousands of environmental protesters had tried to stop the logging by MacBlo and other forestry companies of what was among the last stands of old-growth cedar forests in Canada.

I had been present at those protests, since I knew people on both sides of the dispute, loggers and 'greenies' alike. From my pulpit and at town meetings I had spoken about the need for MacBlo to halt the clear cutting of old-growth cedar.

None of this had gone unnoticed by the company and its partner and perhaps spiritual advisor, the very church that was my employer. But at the time, I had no way of knowing that MacMillan Bloedel had long basked in that sinecure with the United Church of Canada, and was one of its major – read 'grateful' – financial benefactors.

The United Church had earned that endowment. MacBlo had acquired large tracts of native land over time and all over Vancouver Island, land that had been the subject of after-hours enterprise on the part of early missionaries whose supposed mandate had been confined to liberating souls among the Ahousahts: a people, incidentally, who had never received a dime for their own land from church, company or state.

Neither the church nor the company – nor in fact the BC provincial government, which by then had become the largest MacBlo shareholder – wanted this entrepreneurial history to be broadcast, especially considering that the purloined land had hosted one of the more infamous United Church residential schools.

The final twist was lent to the drama by Weyerhaeuser's lusting not only after MacBlo, but the particularly lucrative stands of old-growth cedar of central Vancouver Island, all of which no doubt made mouths water sleeplessly in Seattle.

Time was of the essence. Any scheme to thwart Chief George's claiming of the land had to happen quickly, since, by May of 1993, all land claims negotiations in BC were scheduled to expire. After that, the chiefs would be unable to sign any new deals, with anyone.

When I met him that rainy day, Chief George still hoped that justice would prevail and the land would be returned to its rightful owners, his people. His application for United Church ministry was also in the pipeline then, and had been approved by the church. So the Chief believed that his words would carry weight.

Too much weight, as it turned out. For soon after our meeting, a new, decisive player was called into this drama: a man who would eventually have both Chief George and me expelled from the United Church. His name was Reverend John Cashore, and he had just become the provincial Minister for Aboriginal Affairs.

I had met Cashore once before, ironically, at my premier sermon at First United Church on Vancouver's skid row, where I trained for the ministry and Cashore had been the head guy, just before being elected to the provincial NDP government. Cashore had loved my sermon.

'If all your sermons are that good,' he remarked to me after the service, 'then you have a great career to look forward to in the United Church.'

His words came back to bite him, I suppose, after I started criticizing the Lot 363 deal, and his role in concealing the church's involvement in it.

'Cashore ran interference for the church right down the line,' Bruce explained to me two years later, after my firing.

'He ordered that the United Church be left out of the Lot 363 negotiations completely, despite the wishes of the Ahousahts and the fact that they were the original land-holders who had grabbed it from the Ahousahts. Then he sidelined Earl George by co-opting the other chiefs as partners in a joint venture logging company.'

And developments would get even worse. But that lay months ahead.

10
October 6, 1996 – Vancouver, Canada

'I call Win Stokes.'
It is by now over a month into the delisting hearing. Win Stokes is the second of the Presbytery's witnesses.

After the swearing-in of the witness, Iain Benson faces a perspiring, heavy-set man who seems more nervous than Bob Stiven. Win Stokes, another clergyman, avoids Kevin Annett's fixed stare; he, Stokes, is known to have been the liaison between Presbytery and the Conference during the engineering of Kevin Annett's ouster from St Andrew's United Church.

'Now, Win, I wonder if you can tell us in your own words about the Presbytery's role in removing Kevin Annett as minister at St Andrew's?'
Stokes puffs out a little air.

'Well, I'm not sure exactly. I don't have any personal knowledge of all that, except to say that we didn't have any concern about Kevin until he wrote that letter about the Ahousaht land deal. That was in October of 1994.'
Iain Benson looks like he has swallowed a large jalapeno.

'Mr Stokes, if you would just...'
But Win Stokes stammers on, it seems, Kevin thinks, wishing to expunge any responsibility for Kevin Annett's removal.

'I mean, that's the first time I ever heard of Kevin Annett – it was right after Kevin wrote the letter about the land deal. A provincial government guy told me, "There's no way we can let Kevin Annett

upset the applecart over Lot 363."'
Dr Jessiman actually leaps to his feet, as if a cattle prod has been
applied. He bangs his gavel.

'This is not relevant to Presbytery's line of questioning. I'm going to
instruct the court reporter to strike it from the record.'*During cross-*
examination, Kevin Annett faces Reverend Stokes and ignores
Jessiman's ruling.

'Win, can you elaborate on just who the government guy was who
informed you that I could not be allowed to, I think your expression was
"upset the applecart"? Was that "government guy" by any chance John
Cashore?'*Jessiman again pounds his gavel.*

'This area has already been ruled irrelevant. Since Mr Annett's line of
questioning has no relation to these proceedings, I'm going to declare a
recess for lunch.'*The judicial officer in his role as judge and chief prose-*
cutor now goes into a huddle with Iain Benson and Brian Thorpe.
Then, in his role as impartial judicial officer, he includes once again the
Panel's full quorum in the closed meeting that follows over lunch. As
before, the only person excluded from this luncheon sidebar is Reverend
Kevin Annett.

11
April 1993 – Port Alberni, Canada

By the time of my fateful first meeting with Chief George in Marktosis, the United Church was under enormous pressure to get Lot 363 into the hands of its benefactor MacMillan Bloedel. The urgency was in fattening MacBlo's balance sheet in order to improve the terms of a Weyerhaeuser acquisition that was secretly under way, albeit a rather poorly kept secret.

To add fuel to the fire that was building around me during that spring of 1993, an anti-poverty group that I had helped to organize in the church, known as LIFT (Low Income Folks Together), announced that they were running candidates in the forthcoming municipal elections. And the principal plank in their platform was a program to expropriate MacMillan Bloedel's Tree Farm License and return control over local lands and resources to aboriginal and working people.

From the point of view of Weyerhaeuser, and by inference that of its target MacBlo, not to mention the outriders in church and state, the last thing needed on the local scene was a smart-ass clergyman sounding off weekly in the pulpit about public ownership and stolen native land.

So it was hardly surprising that barely a month after learning the truth from Bruce and Earl George, I received a visitation that in more adventurous dramas is referred to as 'muscle'. In actual fact, this delegation consisted of George Geddes and George Liong, two MacMillan Bloedel employees who were also members of my congregation.

I noted immediately, after they had taken their seats in my church office, that subtlety was not their strong suit.

'We need to talk,' said Geddes, glaring at me while the other George stared at the wall over my head, 'about your bias toward the tree-huggers.'

'Bias?' I asked. It seemed a strange word for a logger.

'You don't really know what you're talking about in your sermons,' he persisted. 'I'd like to take you to a clear-cut area so you can see what really goes on.'I couldn't miss the perhaps veiled threat of being 'taken for a ride', as in a bad Cagney movie. 'I've been to several clear-cuts already,' I told him.

Liong seemed to bristle, but Geddes exploded, 'You don't know the whole story! You should think about that young family of yours, and what they got to lose. I wouldn't want anything bad to happen to you.'

He was red in the face as he got to his feet. I might have laughed at the threatening cliché, but I couldn't. The Hollywood lingo snarled in my little office had too chilling an effect, coming from a guy who had coffee in this same place every Sunday morning.

The two men remained impassive after they stood, and kept staring at me, as if they were waiting for me to react to the threat, or perhaps express some kind of contrition, or agree to go along with them. But I could only stare back, dumbfounded.

I remained sitting behind my desk as they turned and went out without saying anything else.

I didn't mention their threat to my wife, Anne, or to anyone else. Perhaps I should have, because it was all part of a campaign that was slowly building against me.

The chairman of my church board, Fred Bishop, as a former MacBlo executive, made a point of mentioning, on more than one occasion, just how 'concerned' the company was getting about what I was saying about its logging operations, not to mention its monopoly over the local land.

While these threats were pretty explicit, I was still naive in my ignorance of why they were coming at me. This kind of stuff didn't really happen in real life, did it?

12
October 6, 1996 – Vancouver, Canada

After Jon Jessiman concludes his meeting with the Panel, he reconvenes the hearing.

'The preceding testimony,' says Jessiman, 'is completely irrelevant to Presbytery's line of questioning. In fact, let me caution the Panel that anything relating to Reverend Annett's ministering to natives or issues relating to supposed Ahousaht land ownership, or about the residential schools is without significance to these proceedings. I instruct the Panel to disregard all such testimony, and the court reporter to refrain from reproducing it.'
Some of the Panel members are nodding their heads as Kevin Annett rises to his feet.

'Madam Chairperson, I would like to make a formal request that Dr Jessiman be removed as adjudicator of this hearing, on the grounds that he is demonstrating total bias.'
Reverend Mollie Williams appears completely confused.

'In a single statement,' Kevin Annett continues, 'he has acted both as judge and chief prosecutor. Perhaps even chairman of the jury.'
The chairperson straightens her shoulders and appears to be regaining her composure. 'Your motion is out of order.'
'This whole hearing is out of order,' Reverend Annett responds, and sits down.

The chairperson ignores him but rises with a sheet of paper in her hand. 'I would like to announce some new rules relating to these proceedings. First of all, no statements will be allowed or placed into the court record relating to the matter of any Ahousaht land deal or questions relating to Indian land claims.

'In addition, all questions posed to witnesses must be restricted solely to the issue of Reverend Kevin Annett's suitability for ministry. His work with native people has no relevance to this hearing.

'We are also imposing a media blackout on all further proceedings, and no one who is part of or attending this hearing will be allowed to make any statement to the press regarding the hearing.

'Furthermore, anyone passing notes to Reverend Annett or attempting to communicate with him during the hearing will be asked to leave.'
'What, no leg irons?' comments a voice from the crowd of observers, who seem for the most part shocked by the events.

Kevin Annett raises one hand. 'Madam Chairperson, under what authority are you telling us that we are now deprived of our constitutional right of free speech, not to mention dictating how I restrict my line of questioning in these proceedings?'
Reverend Williams does not answer, but turns to look at Dr Jessiman.

'Simply,' says the judicial officer, 'that being an internal review body of an ecclesiastical organization, the Panel has absolute authority to set down whatever rules it deems necessary.'
'Perhaps prior to 1215 and Magna Carta,' says Reverend Annett. 'But are you saying that the United Church and this hearing stand outside the laws of Canada?'
There is no immediate answer from either Jessiman or the Panel chair. Then Jessiman nods at Benson and says,

'Mr Benson, call your next witness.'
'I call Reverend Brian Thorpe.'
Bruce Gunn, who has attended the hearing from its inception and who is present as an advocate for Kevin, addresses the Panel for the first time.

'Madam Chair, Reverend Brian Thorpe is in a total conflict of interest position, since he was the church officer who established this procedure and chose the Panel members.'Dr Jessiman looks at Bruce Gunn as if he is a fly to be squashed. 'That's irrelevant here. We will proceed.'Brian Thorpe is balding and bespectacled, in appearance like the quintessential bureaucrat. He seats his slight frame down in the witness chair. 'Brian, what was your impression of Kevin Annett?' asks Iain Benson. 'And what role did you play in his termination?''I played no role whatsoever in Kevin Annett's termination.'

'Brian,' says Bruce Gunn. 'That is a bald-faced lie.'

Dr Jessiman raps the table. 'Mr Gunn, I insist that you withdraw that remark.''I can reword it, if you like, in stronger terms: both you and Brian Thorpe appointed the Panel, from a short list that you drew up. And Thorpe met with the Presbytery to plan Kevin's firing.''Perhaps,' says Iain Benson, 'you could qualify your statement, Brian?''Actually, I was involved with the Panel in the first instance. Initially I liaisoned between Conference and Presbytery. But then everything was in Presbytery's hands.''And can you now describe your impression of Reverend Annett?'

'I found him not unlike many of our ministers who have a passion for social justice. What Kevin did wasn't that unusual. Kevin's problem, if he has one, is that he wasn't willing to make the compromises we all have had to do to survive in this institution.''Brian,' Dr Jessiman says, 'perhaps you can rephrase that...''I just mean that in the kingdom of God there can be no injustice, no rich or poor. Kevin's only mistake was that he wanted to make that happen here on earth.'

'You got that right,' says Reverend Bruce Gunn. His voice is barely audible.

'We will adjourn,' declares the judicial officer. 'In fact, because of the late date, we will adjourn until the New Year.'

13
1993–1994 – Port Alberni, Canada

I kept to myself everything that Bruce Gunn and Earl George had shared with me on that rainy day in Ahousaht. It bothered me, but I saw no way to do anything about it. My daily work was too engrossing. But the matter would not go away.

For one thing, as my white congregants, mostly loggers and millwrights, began to face more layoffs and even permanent unemployment because of MacBlo's automation of its operations, the white people began to join natives in the food bank lineups in our church's basement. Not only did that commonality of misery dispel many racial stereotypes and bend the color bar that had reigned in Port Alberni, but the issue of who owned the land became a bread-and-butter matter for more of the so-called 'redneck' element in town.

'We can keep pulling drowning people out of the river,' I said in a sermon one Sunday around that time, 'or we can go upstream and find out why they're ending up in the river in the first place.'

Increasing numbers of my people began agreeing with me, and as I continued my open-pulpit policy, their voices began to reverberate alongside native voices in our church sanctuary: cries for justice, and jobs. Needless to say, some of the congregation felt that this 'mixing' of religion and politics was a disruption of what church should be. Our differences were laid bare, in church of all places.

And yet, perhaps because of this stirring-up of what Methodist founder John Wesley once called 'God's Good Trouble', these were the happiest and most productive days of my life until then. My congregation had tripled in size to nearly a hundred souls each Sunday. I was doing what I knew to be right, and doing so honestly and openly, for all to see. And most people responded to this openness, friends and foe alike.

As I looked out every Sunday from my pulpit at the sea of brown and white faces, young and old, rich and poor, an admixture that had not been there when I had arrived, I thought that this was surely what I had been brought there to do: to bring all of these different people together and speak to them of love in action, and show that to them in every moment of my days, so that they could find a deeper commonality, beneath the fracturing of everyday life.

I would look at each of them, seeing God in their smiles and in their sober moments, in their private agonies and unsharable burdens, in their dreams and simple joys and, most movingly, in the delighted laughter of Indian children running alongside white kids, finally, through the halls of our church.

It was all like a last, golden sunset before the darkness descended, but I could not have known this. I did not know what I was unleashing from among those very people who seemed to love and honor me and what I was doing. We were like a happy throng on an ocean cruise, unaware that beneath lay a cargo hold of gunpowder, at that very moment poised to be ignited.

The explosion that was about to rip through my life and so many others' was like an unexpected tornado descending suddenly from out of a calm, blue sky. A whirlwind was about to fall on me and shatter my life: a maelstrom, bringing the deaths of so many hopes, and so many friends – the death, even, of my marriage and family. The death, altogether, of my life as I had known it.

The swelling of my congregation and its apparent enthusiasm over the work I was doing blinded me to the consequences of what I was uncovering, as eyewitnesses to murders and land thefts spoke more and more often from my pulpit. I felt strangely immune to any real danger or consequence from what I was helping to voice, somewhat like a soldier who never really believes that a bullet is meant for him.

I had almost forgotten the tale of the secret land theft committed by my church against the Ahousaht people, as told to me the previous year by Bruce Gunn and Chief Earl George. But the issue would not die, for like a guided missile it pursued me, and impacted during my third year as minister at St Andrew's.

It all began innocuously enough, at a disarmingly banal gathering of my Presbytery in Gold River, BC. The date was October 14, 1994. I was lounging with other bored clergy, listening to humdrum reports on church matters, when the words 'Lot 363' caught my ear.

Our resident reactionary, Oliver Howard, was once again regaling us with his glowing account of the work of early missionaries along the coast, when he let slip how one of them, John Ross, a Presbyterian stalwart launched among the Ahousahts in 1904, had acquired most of their land, including what we now knew as Lot 363 on Flores Island.

'And now the Ahousahts want it back,' said Oliver, with a smirk and a deprecating wave of his hand. 'They want it back, even though it was sold to Ross's grandson in 1953 by our church, and is now in the hands of MacMillan Bloedel. We've tried explaining this to the Ahousaht chiefs, but they refuse to listen to reason and won't even meet with us, which is typical of the Indians.'

His words made my heart leap, because I knew he was lying. Chief George had told me several times that it was the United Church that refused to meet to discuss Lot 363, and that the church could not produce any proof that they had owned the land.

'We never sold it to the church; we couldn't have,' Earl explained. 'We didn't buy or sell land. It's always been Ahousaht land, and the church was wrong to sell it off to MacMillan Bloedel. We want it back.'

Remembering the storm created at a previous Presbytery

meeting by my suggestion that we listen to the Ahousahts, I kept silent during the October gathering. But Oliver's lies and racial slurs could not go unchallenged. I simply couldn't be associated with such deceit. So I typed a letter to the Presbytery officials as soon as I got home.

It was dated October 17, 1994. In it, I said that our church had committed a wrong by stealing and then selling off land that belonged to the Ahousahts against their will. I said that we should admit this wrong and stand by our own policy concerning native land claims, which required that we return all native land in our possession to the indigenous nations from whom we'd taken it. If we did not, I wrote, I would not be able to associate myself with the church on that matter.

I sent off the letter to Presbytery and received no response from them. But within days, my letter was on the desk of the United Church's chief executive officer, Moderator Marion Best, and that of John Cashore, erstwhile United Church minister, and now the Minister of Aboriginal Affairs in the British Columbia government. Three days after that, Presbytery officials, unknown to me, began to meet with my church board to arrange my dismissal from my pulpit.

Having heard nothing from the church, I assumed that the matter was over, and that our officialdom would heed their own policies, and return the land to the Ahousaht people.

14
June 14, 1998 – Vancouver, Canada

Transcript from the Northwest Tribunal into Canadian Indian Residential Schools, sponsored by the United Nations affiliate IHRAAM – 2:06 pm

Tribunal Judge Lydia White Calf – Would you please repeat what you shared with me earlier in our closed session, Helen? Start with who you are.

Witness Helen Morgan – Okay. I'm Helen Morgan from the Burns Lake region and I am a traditional chief and clan mother. I want to go on record that my life was threatened and I was told that if I came here to tell my story I'd be killed.

Tribunal Judge Lydia White Calf – Who threatened you?

Witness Helen Morgan – I don't want to say his name but he works for the top chief in the Carrier-Sekani Tribal Council. This Chief runs the drug trade in that part of the north and traffics in children with the help of the Mounties. He's responsible for a lot of our women who go missing on the Highway of Tears.

Tribunal Judge Lydia White Calf – Why does he want you silent, Helen?

Witness Helen Morgan – Well, for one thing, he was a rapist even when he went to the residential school with me in Kamloops, the Catholic school. He'd inform on all of us when we spoke our languages, then he'd get to do whatever he wanted to us. Now he's the big power up north and everyone is scared to death of him because he has the Mounties and the feds behind him.

Tribunal Judge Lydia White Calf – The government backs this man? Why?

Witness Helen Morgan – Because he delivers for them. He signs away our land and our treaty rights. He made the secret deal with Alcan over its Kemano hydro project that flooded our homes. To steal our land and resources like that, he keeps us all in a state of terror. It used to be the whites that did the genocide on us. Now it's our own people doing it, in partnership with the whites.

15
January 23, 1995 – Port Alberni, Canada

Our last Christmas together as a family had come and gone. The snow was especially deep that winter in the Alberni valley, a fact that delighted my eldest daughter Clare, who was nearly six by then, and her younger sister Elinor, a boisterous two-year-old. The controversy over the Ahousaht land deal had faded from my mind, as the delights of fatherhood and the mounting needs of my burgeoning congregation filled my days.

And so it was with genuine surprise that I received a phone call one evening from Art Anderson, the personnel officer for the BC Conference of the United Church.

'Kevin,' he said. He sounded almost jovial. 'Could you and Anne come over to the church right away?'

'Is there something the matter?' I replied.

'We'll talk when you get here.' He hung up.

Confused but curious, Anne and I arrived to find Anderson sitting in my office. Next to him was Cameron Reid, a gnome-like member of the Comox-Nanaimo Presbytery Executive.

Art Anderson rose and without saying anything, handed me a letter.

The contents hit me like a hammer. It was signed by Phil Spencer, a Presbytery official who had actually attended seminary with me, and whom I considered a friend. It announced that I was being removed immediately as minister at St Andrew's, without providing any reason, and it further set out conditions for my continuance as a United Church minister: I was ordered to submit to a psychiatric evaluation and undergo extensive 'pastoral retraining', without pay, even though I had a family of three to support.

The letter also notified me that my family and I would be

expected to vacate our house in Port Alberni by February 15 – less than a month away, despite the fact that we had a child in kindergarten. All further salary payments to me would be discontinued.

I subsided into a chair beside Anne and handed her the letter. Anne glanced at the letter and within seconds dissolved into tears.

'What is this?' I demanded.

'Just what it says,' Art Anderson said calmly. 'This is for the good of everyone.'

I stared at the man, unable to believe his words. Anne was crying uncontrollably. Both Reid and Anderson looked at her blankly, as they would an insect.

'Why am I being fired?' I asked Anderson.

'It's for the welfare of the congregation.'

'How is it in their welfare to remove their minister?'

'I received complaints about you in writing from five or six people.'

'Which people?'

'I'm not free to say.'

'Can I see these letters?'

'No.'

Later, I was to learn that I couldn't see the letters because they didn't exist. Even though he couldn't actually name what my wrong was, he expected me to play along.

I would also learn later that after he had so shattered Anne and me with my dismissal, Anderson then met with my official board, which had also been suddenly convened in the sanctuary of the church. In that meeting, of which I was unaware, Anderson distributed copies of my dismissal letter to everyone present, pointing out to them the church's demand on me for a psychiatric evaluation, and adding: 'Everyone needs to read this.'

I wrote later in my diary that Anne and I huddled together that night like rape victims. I was being violated and slaughtered in front of my entire congregation.

I should have realized what was happening earlier when, following the Presbytery meeting when I wrote my Lot 363 letter, I had been asked in December to attend a kangaroo meeting where three church members acting on their own authority delivered an ultimatum to me to discontinue operation of the food bank in the church, stop preaching about social justice, and stop visiting 'non-members' (their term for Indians), or face immediate firing. But their ultimatum had never been followed through on, until Anderson appeared.

Faced with this realization, I nevertheless found it impossible to play ball with Art Anderson. I knew that if I went along with these demands on me, I would be not only betraying everything that I had tried to build in Port Alberni, but would be helping to conceal the crimes that had been committed in the residential schools. For clearly, those crimes were on the mind of the United Church.

Two days later, Anderson raised the pressure on me with a letter threatening in writing to 'defrock' me permanently from ministry altogether if I didn't agree to their demands 'no later than February 9, 1995', which, not accidentally, was the very day that the local RCMP were scheduled to open their 'official investigation' into the Alberni residential school. Obviously, the church wanted me long gone before that inquiry began.

That's when I knew for certain that something much bigger was at stake than a minister who supposedly wouldn't 'fit' with his congregation.

Every United Church official I dealt with exhibited the same cruel intransigence towards me and my situation: I had to go along with everything they demanded or be out on the street within the month.

At first, none of them would have anything to do with me, refusing to answer my phone calls and desperate requests to sit down and iron out our differences.

There was even unexplainable sadism. A day after my firing,

the Presbytery official who had signed my dismissal letter, Phil Spencer, called Anne at our home. Clearly, he had been briefed that Anne was the weak link in our chain.

'Kevin had this coming to him!' he screamed into the phone after Anne answered it. Perplexed, she asked if we couldn't work things out.

'It's too late for that!' he yelled back, chortling aloud, since he appeared to have been drinking. 'So go ahead and sue us! A lot of people have tried suing the church and they've never won!'

This insane kind of terrorizing had a method to it, as was exhibited more clearly in the months that followed, in which every pressure tactic in the book was thrown at me – including the church's subversion of my marriage and theft of my children.

Anne was terrified of what was going on, and had confided a lot of her fears to a local counselor who was friends with Fred Bishop and other local church officials. Apparently, the counselor violated his professional oath of confidentiality, and divulged Anne's fears to Bishop, who passed on this vital information to the men who would fire me – and who knew exactly where to strike.

Barely a month after I was fired, these men approached Anne and offered to pay for her divorce if she left me and provided them information on my plans. Anne agreed to do so, and in secret, amidst our collapsing life, she made arrangements to leave me and deprive me of my children.

I did not suspect a thing at the time. As naively as I had expected justice from the church, I assumed that she and I would survive the whole ordeal. We had two small daughters to protect, after all, and ten years together.

Incapable of even imaging the betrayal that would soon strike me so close to home, I struggled to negotiate with the church and hold together my ministry with those who most needed it. For the very day that I was fired, in the middle of winter, Fred Bishop and the church 'old guard' had closed our Loaves and Fishes food bank, denying 300 mostly native families of the food they needed to survive every month.

The United Church claimed, at the time, that it couldn't afford the $1,200 every month needed to feed these people. But the next year, they didn't hesitate to come up with over $250,000 to throw me out of my profession and livelihood.

Soon after my firing, my supporters had scattered in fear, and native families and the poor had been forced out of the congregation, which eventually collapsed back to the score of older white folks who had greeted me three years previously. St Andrew's Church, in fact, was forced to close down a few years after my departure and merge with the other United Church in town. If only a Pyrrhic victory, this collapse was at least a sign of what happens to people when they kill the best in themselves, and among themselves.

The brutality of this time also taught me something else: about the nature of the church I had been part of, and the truth of what residential school survivors had told me. For, up to my firing, I still didn't quite believe that my church had committed mass murder. Indeed, I could not ultimately have accepted the stories of murder and torture in church schools revealed to me by survivors had I not experienced personally the brutal inhumanity of the church and its officers.

When I saw the cold vacuum in the eyes of Art Anderson and Phil Spencer over my children's suffering, when I felt their indifference and cruelty personally, I knew with sudden blinding clarity that, of course, the same church could have killed children with a darker skin color. For if they could do this to one of their own, I thought, what might be possible in their treatment of all those 'other' people?

There is no quantitative measuring of the evil that contemplates the destruction of another. 'One who has taken a single life is as one who has killed an entire people,' says the Jewish Talmud. But the corollary to this wisdom, of course, is that 'One who has saved a single life is as one who has redeemed an entire world.'

Both truths were now laid bare to me. And I had to choose which one I was to serve.

16
January 1994 – Port Alberni, Canada

A Requiem for Mark

The lives and deaths of so many people around him suggest a fundamental question: since Jesus seems to have been preoccupied with the poor and wretched of the earth, what is it that they – like Victor Hugo's misérables – can teach avowed Christians? And what value can be discerned, let alone held up as inescapable, in a single human life, and death?

He finds a supreme example in a young man called Mark Angus, who dies by his own hand in Port Alberni early in that pivotal year.

He knows little of Mark at first, simply as someone who for more than a year helps with the operation of his church's food bank and is always on hand when there is a need. Mark is one of the first to stand up in church and speak honestly about his own life, asking God and each of them for help with his addictions.

Mark's readiness to ask for help causes most people to draw back from him. The usual boundaries and evasions don't appear to bother him. He seems to see the truth as it is, not least about himself, and he has no hesitation in expressing it.

Perhaps it is this crystal clarity in Mark that leads him to kill himself on a cold January day in a hotel room two blocks from the church. It is as if everything seems so clear to him that he is unable to find a self-delusion in which to hide, to absent himself from the stark nightmare around and within him.

For an entire week before that, Kevin strives with him to stave off his death wish, after Mark comes to him just after Christmas and announces that he wants to end his life.

'But why?'

Kevin is hard-put to conceal his anger, but more honestly his grief, that Mark would ignore the good work they are doing together; grief that he, Mark, would abandon their mission, and their friendship.

'The reason is there is no reason, for anything,' Mark says calmly. 'So what if we feed people who are hungry? Tomorrow they'll just be as poor as ever. One day they'll die. It's all pointless, ultimately.'
'I don't agree,' Kevin says, not really believing his own words.
'Is God here? I've never experienced him. I try to every day, every night, and he never answers.'
'That isn't how it works. We make our own answers, every day.'
'I'm tired of having to do that all the time. I'm just tired of everything.'

Kevin stands up and paces his office. Outside the window, the snow is piling up.
'What about your son, over in England? You tell me he's only six. He'll never know you if you end it now.'
Mark nods, sadly, but says nothing.

'I'm not going to let you do this, Mark!' Kevin exclaims at him, and at the close darkness.

Mark smiles.
'I'm gonna miss you too, Kev.'

Then he pauses and looks at his friend more closely.
'You're the one I worry about. I'm gonna be okay. I know that. But you'll have to stay here, in this place. It's targeted you. It hates you for pulling back its mask. It hides in this church, and you and I both see it for what it is.'

He makes a strange gesture just then, like a dog shaking itself.

'I can't hack it anymore. It's too big. But you're a marked man, Kev, because you won't back down, even when you face losing everything, and everyone. It knows that, so it will never stop attacking you.'
Kevin nods, knowing it's all true.

Mark's voice suddenly grows stronger.

'You've got only one defense, Kev. Stop turning your pulpit over to others. That's not your purpose. You think more of them than you do about why you've been put here, among us. You've got to tell them the truth!'
What matters suddenly is not Mark's resolve, but rather that he is a messenger who has accepted his purpose, even as he knows his own finality.

A week later, it is over.

There is a eulogy in front of the fifty or so who attend Mark's funeral service that morning. Kevin leads them in a brief prayer, and then stands in front of Mark's coffin.

'I found Mark in his hotel room, a few days ago. He had been dead for two days, just lying there, all alone. He died alone. He was ignored by most of us, even those of us who called him friend. So when I thought about how he lived, and died, I realized how ineffectual we all are, caring about God only when we need something, using others and calling that "life".
'Mark was tired of the way we live, of what our culture has become, and he couldn't be part of it anymore. That's what he told me, just over a week ago. He was a man of substance, and so he couldn't live in our world or church any longer.

'Another man we pretend to follow showed us the truth about the world, and he was killed for it. We can't tolerate pure people among us, maybe because their brightness shows up our lives too clearly. But even when we drive them from our midst, their light persists among us. And it can still change us, long after they are gone.

'The Jews call these pure ones the Lamed Waf, or the "Just Souls", who suffer for humanity, who redeem all of us in God's eyes by their capacity to hold the divine suffering in their own selves, and thereby prevent our destruction. Mark was one of these just souls. He had no choice; he was born one. And that's why I think I tried to know him.
'The Jewish Talmud teaches that Jesus was one of many "just souls", while our Bible depicts him as the "only son of God".

'The Nuu-Chah-Nulth people, whose descendants are here among us today, long ago came to believe, like the Gnostic Christians, that there was an inner message imparted by Jesus to his closest followers, including Mary Magdalene and Thomas. The Nuu-Chah-Nulth people believe that, long before the Europeans arrived here, they too were visited by Christ, in the form of a woman, who considered the west coast people worthy of receiving the inner message of her gospel.

'It isn't important whether we believe that or not. But the Gnostics were attacked and destroyed by the Christian church in the two centuries after Jesus, because their teachings opposed official Christianity. In the same way, the local people here were almost exterminated by Christianity. Is this merely coincidence?

'Those other Christians believed that spiritual ignorance, not sin, was humankind's chief enemy, and that inner, personal wisdom was the path to salvation, not the atoning sacrifice of Christ and the sacramental life of the church.

'So we all have this choice: whether to believe in Jesus' foundational *teaching, that "the kingdom of heaven is within you", or, on the contrary, to believe along with orthodox Christianity that "the kingdom of heaven is within the church".*

'Just before he died, Mark told me that whatever evil was hiding in the Christian church was somehow being unmasked by the work he and I and others were doing here in the valley. He said this Thing hated us for doing so, and wouldn't rest until we were all destroyed. Perhaps it started with Mark. But it's also claimed many other innocents, and one day it may claim me, too.

'But that doesn't matter, for it's not the final word, any more than our church's genocide of the people here has been. What matters is that we each see the choice set out for us, between the lie and the truth – between Christ and the falseness erected in his name. And I hope you will see how Mark, not with his death but with his life, made that choice; and how his choice is asking each one of us to also choose.'

17
1995 – Port Alberni and Vancouver, Canada

After months of fruitless negotiations with Presbytery, which were ultimately sabotaged by Jon Jessiman and other church officials, my family and I were destitute, since I was prohibited from working anywhere else in the church. Anne, our children and I were forced to move away from Port Alberni in July of 1995, and live with relatives in Vancouver.

My heartbreak at leaving the Alberni valley, and so many friends, was made all that more difficult by Anne's increasing withdrawal from me. Still not realizing her plan to divorce me after her secret agreement with the church, I enrolled at the University of British Columbia (UBC) in September of 1995, to pursue a doctoral program in native studies. My hope was still to return to active ministry, but in the meantime to research the history and anthropology of the system that had brought about my family's suffering – and that of so many native people.

Still ordained yet unable to seek employment, I experienced an odd sense of freedom when I began my studies at UBC, despite our pressing poverty and dislocation. With nothing required of me, I could deepen my study of the west coast Indian residential schools, drawing on my practical fieldwork among native people and a wealth of archival material just acquired by the Koerner Library at UBC.

But before that happened, I was wrenched back into my former life in Port Alberni by a collect phone call. It came from a homeless man named John Sargent whom I had come to know well and had befriended, and who had been active in my church.

'You'd better get your ass over here, Kev,' John announced. 'Cecilia Joseph just burned to death in a slum fire.'

Cecilia was a quiet, friendly woman whom I had met and seen regularly at our Loaves and Fishes food bank. She had first appeared one Wednesday morning to collect food for her family, but had stayed all day, helping to bag food and look after kids, and talk to me about her life.

Cecilia once showed me the scars on her arms and legs from the long needles the nuns had shoved into the tortured little girl she had been at the Christie residential school at Tofino, out on the west coast. And she had witnessed her five-year-old cousin beaten to death by a priest there.

Now it was Cecilia who was dead. She had met her end horribly when the one room she rented from a slum landlord named Gus Frigstad was immolated when the building caught fire. The room lacked a door handle and a fire alarm, so she was unable to escape.

I was asked by Cecilia's family to conduct her funeral, so I took a ferry to Port Alberni the following morning.

By the time I arrived, Cecilia's family had contacted every church in the Alberni valley. Unanimously, their clergymen had refused to help, and had even disallowed the use of their churches, once they discovered for whom the funeral service was intended.

Included in this group were the two United Churches in town. Kathleen Hogman, my successor at St Andrew's, had told Cecilia's people that the sanctuary was being used at that time. That was later proven to be a lie. A different wrinkle was provided by Ryan Knight, the minister of Port Alberni's First United Church and a former classmate and friend of mine. That friendship, of course, had evaporated promptly with my firing.

'That's not possible,' he lied to Cecilia's brother when he called, 'because Kevin Annett is not allowed to use any United Church facility.'

'That's not the first time he's turned us down,' commented Cecilia's brother. 'Our grandparents tried to have our kids baptized at that church and the same minister refused to do it. He said Indians had to go to their own church.'

Nobody, it seemed, desegregated Port Alberni with impunity, although I had tried. But my work at St Andrew's had only served to set off alarm bells among the local 'god-fearing' white population.

The Odd Fellows Lodge of Port Alberni turned out to be less odd than their religious fellow citizens. We were allowed to use their hall for Cecilia's service. More than a hundred people attended. As I had done at St Andrew's, following a brief tribute to Cecilia's gentle kindness, I opened up the meeting to anyone who cared to speak.

The speakers were led by an older man, an uncle of Cecilia's, who leaned on a cane, but whose words pierced all of us. For the first time, the name of Alfred Caldwell, a former principal and murderer of a child at the Alberni residential school, was revealed.

'Cecilia here wouldn't hurt a fly, but now she's dead,' wheezed the old man. 'She was killed by a white man's greed. It's always been that way for us. Up at the residential school here, we saw a lot of children die. We know about Principal Caldwell and how he killed that girl one night. We can't let this go on anymore.'

But more was said. It was Jack McDonald, the president of the local Metis Society, who, after speaking at Cecilia's funeral, proposed the organization of a Tribunal to investigate Cecilia's death, and the murders in the Alberni residential school. The following year, Harriet Nahanee and I were to pick up Jack's idea and act on it.

But in the meantime, the Cecilias kept dying.

18
March 6, 1997 – Vancouver, Canada

Now seven months into the hearing, a nervous and desperate Iain Benson makes an announcement:
'I would like to introduce as evidence certain letters that go to the central point at issue, which is Kevin Annett's unfitness as a minister at St Andrew's.'

With a flourish, he removes several sheets of paper from his briefcase.

'This unsolicited letter was sent to me from the United Church's Personnel Committee. I can read it if you wish, but I can perhaps save time, prior to entering it into the record, by simply saying that the Committee was unanimously in favor of Kevin's dismissal.'Kevin speaks up.
'I've never seen a copy of that letter. Is this evidence?'
Jessiman ignores him as Benson continues with zeal.

'Next, there is a letter dated in early June of 1995 from Art Anderson, the personnel officer for the BC Conference, in which he indicates that the church had had concerns about Kevin Annett for some time. In fact, he states that he recommended that the church should prevent Mr Annett from working elsewhere – on the recommendation of Dr Jon Jessiman.'
Benson slows as he reaches the final sentence, as if wishing that he hadn't said it.

Shocked, yet pleased, Kevin speaks up again.

'The Panel should know that this letter's statement by Dr Jessiman, advising Art Anderson and Presbytery to break off all negotiations

with me, came at a time when Presbytery was concluding an agreement with me that would have allowed me at least to retain my standing as a minister. So Dr Jessiman, by his own admission, sabotaged these negotiations.' The enormity of this fact seems to sink in with everyone in the room. Benson looks sick, realizing what his zeal to sink Kevin has caused.

Bruce Gunn stands and says: 'Madam Chairperson, because our supposedly unbiased judicial officer has just been proven to have been the instigator of this hearing, demonstrating a gross conflict of interest, I must move that Dr Jessiman be removed as judicial officer for the Panel and this hearing.' Reverend Williams looks confused. She turns helplessly to Dr Jessiman who announces, with staggering impropriety, 'I suggest that we adjourn to consider this motion.'
After reconvening the hearing, Chairperson Mollie Williams opens the session with the reading of a prepared statement.

'The Panel denies the request by Reverend Annett, and it furthermore expresses its total confidence in Dr Jessiman's neutrality and integrity in all matters pertaining to the hearing. The proceedings will now continue.'
Kevin Annett raises one hand.

'In which case, Madam Chairman, I would like Bruce Gunn to read into the record a statement on my behalf.' Reverend Gunn rises.

'That statement is as follows: "In light of the Panel's wrongful denial of our motion to have Dr Jon Jessiman step down as judge of these proceedings, since he is clearly in a grave and obvious conflict of interest, I, Reverend Kevin Annett, have no choice but to withdraw from these proceedings.
"Further participation in this hearing by me may compromise my standing in any future legal action against the United Church. I do not wish to appear complicit in or in agreement with the fraudulent, unfair

and biased nature of these proceedings.

"I therefore remove myself from this hearing, and will appeal its proce-dures to a civil court." 'Kevin Annett and Bruce Gunn then walk out of the hearing. As they are exiting the church hall, the Panel chairperson, Mollie Williams, calls after them. She pronounces what many of those attending view as the only truthful statement she has made during the entire proceedings: 'Bruce, Kevin, if you leave this hearing you'll both face dire consequences!'

19
December 18, 1995 – Vancouver, Canada

A medieval mystic named Magister Eckhart once described the actions of angels on his shadowed soul as feeling at first like the burning tongs of demons, tearing him apart. Thus did I begin to experience the wrenching liberation of my compromised life, as my old life began to end for good soon after our leaving Port Alberni.

The pivotal moment came in mid-December, at a protest rally I staged outside the United Church headquarters in Vancouver. It was there that I first met a defiant native woman named Harriet Nahanee.

Like all of my people, I thought that I understood who we were as Canadians, until I met people like Harriet – and until my own life began to unravel. I seriously doubt that, had I remained on the safe side of a job, livelihood and family, I would ever have learned the truth about Canada and Christianity – even if I had met people like Harriet.

My unlearning began in earnest not when I encountered residential school survivors or uncovered the records of their murder, but when I lost my own children. My unlearning had to begin in my own shattered heart.

During a single week in December of 1995, I met Harriet, and my wife Anne left me. These two, not unrelated, events happened because I refused to cooperate with the United Church in my own destruction.

Psychological warfare is not intended to make sense. It's designed to confuse and demoralize the targeted person, so as to keep that person incapable of action. But the deliberate and constant nature of the assaults against me revealed from the beginning that the church's agenda was simple. As one sitting on the truth of their lie, and their crime, I had to be crushed.

The ultimate means of completing my destruction was to coordinate their attacks on me with the help of Anne, who received the green light to divorce me from the church during the very week that I met Harriet and we were both quoted in the pages of the *Vancouver Sun* about the murders of children at the United Church's Alberni Indian Residential School.

For Harriet Nahanee was an eyewitness to a killing.

Harriet was in her sixties when I met her outside the United Church office at our protest: a slight wraith of a woman with gray hair caught in a ragged pony tail, dark close-set eyes above a straight firm mouth always set and humorless. It was like the permanent scar across her adulthood: the searing memory of her witness as a child – the murder of another child.

Unbending and relentless, as long as I knew her until her sudden death, and probable murder, in early 2007, she would state her creed against society: 'We don't need healing – we need to bring the bastards to justice.'

Harriet had heard of my protest and decided it was time to tell what she knew to the press. Undeterred by niceties, she didn't even introduce herself to me and the cluster of friends who picketed the church office with me. Instead, she began loudly regaling reporters with what she had seen on Christmas eve when she was ten years old, huddled under a flight of stairs at the Alberni residential school.

From that spot, hiding from her rapist, Harriet had seen the criminal appear, and kick to her death another little girl: fourteen-year-old Maisie Shaw of Port Renfrew, BC.

The rapist and murderer was Principal Albert Caldwell.

She said so to the *Vancouver Sun* reporter and other media who came to my protest, which had been called to highlight my wrongful firing by the church. But now the protest had become something else, as it was meant to be.

Harriet's story made headlines in the *Vancouver Sun* the next day, the first public eyewitness account of a residential school murder.

The stakes were suddenly much larger than a congregation's squabbling over a nosy minister. And nobody realized this better than the United Church of Canada.

Two days later, a second eyewitness, Archie Frank, was quoted in the *Vancouver Sun* as saying that Alfred Caldwell had beaten another child to death for taking a prune out of a jar. Suddenly, the United Church of Canada was accused of homicide, and officials like Brian Thorpe saw, rightly, that I was the cause of the exposure. So, possibly that same day, Thorpe contacted my wife Anne and pressed her to launch her divorce action against me.

I stumbled over sudden proof of this tag-team operation one morning just before Anne left me, in late December of 1995. As I was sorting through family papers in one of our cupboards, I came across an unfamiliar yellow file folder. It bore the stenciled name 'Brian Thorpe', who, you may recall, had also arranged my firing by the Presbytery.

'What's this?' I asked Anne, who was standing near me.

She grabbed it out of my hand and looked away, but I had seen fear in her eyes.

'It's nothing!' she blurted out as she hurried from the room.

At the time, I was so totally distracted by the attacks against me, and by my struggle to support my family, that I was incapable of connecting the dots. The very church official who had arranged my firing was in open communication with my wife. And even clearer proof came the following month, after Anne had served divorce papers on me, when the church acknowledged that their lawyer Iain Benson, who would lead the campaign to defrock me in 1996, had met with Anne and her lawyer on two occasions to plan her divorcing me.

Within the week of the protest where I met Harriet Nahanee,

Anne had vanished with my children, after announcing to me on Christmas Eve that she was seeking a divorce. So death struck Maisie Shaw and my family on the same hallowed eve, and at the hands of the same power.

20
March 7, 1997 – Vancouver, Canada

Unbelievers deserve not only to be separated from the Church ... but also to be severed from the world by death ... If the unbeliever is still stubborn, the Church, no longer hoping for his conversion, looks to the salvation of others, and delivers him to the secular tribunal to be exterminated from the world by death.

Thomas Aquinas, *Summa Theologica* (II), 'Should Heretics Be Tolerated?'

The professional extinguishing of Kevin Annett proceeds as did any medieval auto-da-fé, like clockwork, according to the time-honored church tradition of publicly humiliating and then executing heretics.

The delisting Panel disregards Kevin Annett's departure from its midst, and proceeds as if it retained legitimacy. The Panel convenes the following day, even though Kevin Annett and all his supporters have withdrawn from the hearing. Solicited letters obtained by Iain Benson that are highly critical of Kevin Annett, and which come only from church officials, are introduced as bona fide evidence into the court record, while thirty-eight letters of support for Kevin from former parishioners are barred from the record.

The Panel is instructed by Dr Jessiman to bring in a verdict against Reverend Kevin Annett, and accept Presbytery's motion to expel him from ordained ministry in the United Church.
And with that, Kevin Annett is stripped of his livelihood and his public reputation.

The following day, Kevin receives a couriered letter from G.R. Schmitt, a lawyer with the Ferguson Gifford law firm in Vancouver. It warns him that if he makes any public statement about the United Church of Canada or its dealings with native people, or concerning the events of his delisting hearing, he will face a lawsuit.

Kevin ignores the letter.

The delisting Panel's final report makes no reference to any of Kevin Annett's arguments, nor to Lot 363, nor to aboriginal people; nor does it contain reference to any of the objections made by Kevin Annett or Bruce Gunn throughout the hearing. Instead, it describes Reverend Annett as a chronic malcontent who had alienated the congregation, and has been expelled from the church for the sake of its 'peace and welfare'.
The Panel's final report on Kevin Annett is placed on the national website of the United Church of Canada, where it continues to beguile the uninformed.
British Columbia's Attorney General, Ujjal Dosanjh, in response to twenty-two letters of protest from people who attended the hearing, refuses to intervene or to review the findings of the hearing, on the grounds that 'the internal procedures of the Church fall outside the jurisdiction of this department'.
Officially, then, the church is deemed to be above the law.

In the aftermath of the United Church's delisting of Kevin Annett: MacMillan Bloedel continues to own Lot 363 and its old-growth cedar forest, having purchased it from the United Church for more than $1,000,000. In 1999, MacMillan Bloedel is acquired by the Weyerhaeuser Company of Seattle in the largest corporate takeover in British Columbia history.

Ujjal Dosanjh, the Attorney General of British Columbia and cabinet colleague of former United Church minister John Cashore, later becomes Premier of that province and eventually a federal cabinet minister.
Church official Brian Thorpe is elevated to national prominence as

coordinator for aboriginal affairs in the United Church of Canada. Art Anderson, Bob Stiven, Win Stokes and others who acted against Kevin Annett take early retirement, on full pension.

Chief Earl Maquinna George is denied ordination as a United Church minister, and retires to Flores Island, where he dies in obscurity several years later.

The other elders in the Ahousaht Tribal Council share in the joint venture company created by MacMillan Bloedel, and eventually acquire full shares of the company, known as Ilsaak Ltd., which continues to clear-cut old-growth forests in the Clayoquot basin, presumably with 'aboriginal respect for the land'.

Reverend Bruce Gunn receives no compensation for his advocacy and support of Reverend Kevin Annett. Rather, following the chairperson's warning, he is forced by the Comox-Nanaimo Presbytery to resign because of his 'unsuitability as a minister' on Flores Island. He is divorced by his wife, and later moves to a remote area of northern British Columbia, where he finds employment as a counselor.

As for Kevin Annett, like Ulysses, he continues to wander on a quest as yet unclear, alone yet determined, condemned by the gods yet undeterred.

21
September 1995 – Vancouver, Canada

On the eve of my divorce and defrocking, as my soon-to-be-shattered family and I recovered from the shock of our Port Alberni departure, I sought solace and refuge on the quiet campus of the University of BC where I had grown up. As when I was a teenager, the silent library stacks and volumes brought me a peace only rivaled by the dense forests that surrounded the campus. It was in this place of recovery that I discovered the evidence that would prompt me along the path of a new life.

As I began to pursue my doctoral research, I was led one morning to the microfilm section of the old library, where, to my first surprise, I discovered that the history of the Indian residential school crimes had not been a well-kept secret at all. That history had been written, acknowledged and reported in both government reports and the public media for almost a century.

On that fall morning, barely a month into my program, a heading under 'Department of Indian Affairs' caught my eye, and suddenly I discovered that the entire record of Indian residential schools in British Columbia had been acquired by the UBC library system that very year. There before me lay seventy-seven spools of microfilm containing a treasure trove of explosive evidence about what had gone on in the west coast residential schools since 1890.

I found these records to be an incredible goldmine of information, containing school records, Indian Agent reports about conditions in the schools, and petitions and complaints from native elders and parents about, among other things, the deaths and suffering of students.

The general tone of the government and public attitude at the time can best be illustrated by reference to the federal Superintendent of Indian Affairs during the early twentieth century, Duncan Campbell Scott, a sort of fin-de-siècle Renaissance man in Ottawa circles. Beloved by most Canadians as a poet who still graces the pages of CanLit, Scott was also sometime President of the Royal Society of Canada and was festooned with honorary doctorates from the universities of Toronto and Queens.

When he wasn't writing poetry extolling the beauty of Canada's wilderness and the noble native people who inhabited it, for the emolument of polite society in Ontario, he was known to have dashed off inter-office memos of a more practical if equally lyric nature. Typical is the following prose selection which he composed in 1910:

> If these savages will not come into our residential schools voluntarily, they must be forced to come by the law. The churches will have it no other way. It is true that the Indian children die in our schools at a much higher rate from tuberculosis, but such is in keeping with the policy of our department, which is committed to the final solution of the Indian problem.

Notwithstanding the lyric nature of Scott's prose, it was a surprising discovery, since I had thought that Heinrich Himmler had invented that final *bon mot*, in referring to the Jews.

Compared with such a departmental directive by his superior, the concern of one Dr Peter Bryce, the Chief Medical Inspector for the department, stands in obvious contrast, and suggests that Dr Bryce's days may have been numbered. Indeed, Bryce was subsequently removed from his position. Three years earlier, after conducting a personal inspection tour of most of the western residential schools, Bryce had written in his report:

'I believe the conditions are being deliberately created in our Indian residential schools to spread infectious disease. The death rate often exceeds 50%. This is a national crime.'

This enormous death rate, which spanned decades, was attributed by Bryce to a regular practice in the residential schools of 'housing the sick with the healthy indiscriminately, and never treating them for Tuberculosis or any other contagious disease'.

Later I would begin sharing this evidence with lawyers for the native people suing the churches and government, and the United Church's hatred of me would escalate accordingly. In fact, within two days of the first lawsuit against the church being announced, in February of 1996, the United Church of Canada decided to proceed with my formal 'defrocking'. But that was still months away.

The obscure and fading report by Dr Peter Bryce gave me the first verified evidence that the residential schools had been an exercise in deliberate genocide – that over half of all the children in Indian residential schools had died every year from their deliberate exposure to communicable diseases, with the full knowledge and sanction of church and state in Canada.

The report's author, Dr Bryce, was not a dissident radical but an establishment official who even proceeded so far as to claim that the churches that ran the residential schools were deliberately killing off children, concealing their crime, and fudging school records to protect the perpetrators.

But the astounding fact for me was that at that time his findings had even been reported in front-page articles in two of the (then and now) major Canadian daily newspapers – the *Ottawa Citizen* and the *Montreal Gazette* – during November of 1907. To share a phrase of Dr Noam Chomsky, the truth of our homegrown Canadian genocide had literally been 'flushed down the memory hole'.

One of my other important discoveries in the microfilm

87

archives at UBC was a single document known as the 'Application for Admission' form into the Indian residential schools, which every aboriginal parent was forced to sign, under pain of imprisonment, as it was interpreted to them by the Royal Canadian Mounted Police officers who came to collect their children.

The 'application' form surrendered legal guardianship over their own children to the residential school principal – invariably a clergyman – under the general direction of the federal Minister of Mines and Resources.

Suddenly, more than one wall came tumbling down for me: for this document not only proved that the churches were liable for the crimes and damages in these schools, as legal guardian of the children, but it demonstrated graphically how and why all manner of crimes could have been committed and concealed for so many years, in a clear joint operation conducted by church and state.

I quickly became a denizen of the dusty shelves of UBC library, and went nearly blind trying to decipher century-old handwriting. But the more I learned, the more I felt the need to report my findings in my graduate studies seminars at the University.

'You're not suggesting that it was deliberate?' said Jean Barman, one of my professors, on the first occasion that I produced Dr Bryce's records in a native studies class. That report indicated a 50% mortality rate in Alberta residential schools.

'Well,' I said, 'how could so many of them have died, so consistently over so many years, in schools run by every religious denomination, unless it was the result of a policy and a deliberate practice?'

Confident that pure reasoning would prevail over denial, I even pointed out that it was not inconsistent with a policy adopted earlier in the U S Congress, when an Act was introduced in 1870 with the express purpose of annihilating the Navajo

Nation. Or, as a closer geographical example, with the Gradual Civilization Act of 1857 in Upper Canada (now Ontario), which tried legally to extinguish any separate native identity or nationhood.

As time went on within my classes and seminars, the looks on the white faces around the seminar table every time I raised the subject told me that I had breached the limits of scholarly discourse. Totally unacceptable, even at the postgraduate level, was the notion that colonial Canada could have been capable of even a relatively modest genocide.

As with my previous experience in the church, I gradually became a sort of pariah around my department. I found that I was becoming cautiously avoided by all the career-conscious graduate students. All of them knew that my thesis subject was concerned with the United Church Indian residential schools on the west coast of British Columbia.

'I think you've chosen a dangerous research topic,' said my department chairman, Patricia Vertinsky, some time later, when she called me into her office. 'I'd suggest you give it a little more thought before you get too far into your dissertation.'

It all seemed very confusing to me at the time. After all, was the University not a center and a bastion of free thought and expression?

But once again, I had the feeling that I had stumbled across some shameful family secret that everyone knew about but would never discuss, or even acknowledge to themselves. I began to realize that so deeply imbedded in our society was the 'organized religion' cultural addiction that, even in this group – most of whom as enlightened academics were not practicing Christians, much less churchgoers – there was an inability to challenge their own irrational assumption, so contradicted by the historical evidence, that Christian churches were incapable of murder.

All my colleagues seemed to agree that I was someone to be

instinctively avoided. And those rare exceptions, fellow students who supported my work, soon found themselves the target of not-very-subtle pressure to dissociate themselves from me.

The situation for me was even worse than I at first realized. I did not know at first that one of the senior faculty members in my department, Murray Elliot, was also an official on the United Church's executive body in British Columbia. In fact, I eventually learned that he had actually sat on the committee that voted to begin 'delisting' proceedings against me.

From Port Alberni, I had proceeded out of the frying pan and into the fire, just when I thought I had won a very painful and costly freedom.

The crowning blow came when I learned that Murray Elliot was also the faculty member in charge of determining which of the graduate students in our department would receive funding and, equally important, teaching assistantships. It didn't require an Einstein to guess what bright-eyed ex-minister would not be receiving monetary encouragement during his two-year PhD program.

And sure enough, that's exactly what transpired. Despite my first-class grade average, I became the first student in depart-mental history with such marks to be denied any funding for two consecutive years. Unable to pay my tuition, I was never able to complete my PhD.

But Murray Elliot did more than sabotage my funding and my studies: he also began actively to disparage my name around the department, claiming that I had been a 'terrible minister and father', and even telling people that 'his thesis will never get published'.

One day, Elliott even demanded in a rage that a certain graduate student named Helen Papuni – one of the few who were giving me the time of day – remove from her office door a newspaper article sympathetic to me. Elliot even threatened to have Helen expelled if she failed to do so, declaring to her, 'Kevin will never finish his degree, and neither will you if you're not careful.'

'It doesn't make any sense,' said my thesis advisor, a rather nice guy named Don Wilson. It was the afternoon when the results of graduate student assistance were announced and my name was conspicuous by its absence.

'You have a grade-point average of 88% in your course work so far,' Don said, shaking his head worriedly. 'Anyone in this department's graduate studies program with a first-class average like yours has always been a shoo-in for graduate funding, usually with a teaching assistantship as well. I've never seen anything like this.'

Soon after, Don offered to appeal my case to the chairman of the department. And yet, the next week, he came to me, as white as a sheet, and told me he couldn't chair my thesis committee any longer. Don avoided my stares after that, and in fact took early retirement the following year.

After I was forced from the department, I charged Murray Elliot before a university ethics committee with interfering with my academic freedom, and being in a gross conflict of interest as a United Church official and the departmental financial officer who decided my funding. I even addressed a letter to that effect to the University's Board of Governors.

That was an exercise in futility. Without even investigating the case, UBC official Dennis Pavlich announced to me within a few days of receiving my complaint that Murray Elliot was 'in no conceivable way' in a conflict of interest, and my complaint was rejected.

Such a rapid disposal of the whole affair by the university administration made me realize that more than the church and its agents were involved.

For many years, one of the University's largest benefactors, and continuously represented on the Board of Governors, was my old corporate nemesis MacMillan Bloedel and corporate colleagues such as Interfor, Crown Zellerbach and Weyerhaeuser. More than one UBC Chancellor had also been senior executives with those same forestry companies.

As Bruce Gunn had exclaimed a year earlier, 'Kev, you sure know how to pick your enemies!'

Seemingly thrown out in the cold once again, I discovered that it was precisely at such moments that new doors were being opened for me, so that the truth of Canada's holocaust would not be lost. And through one of these doors at that time walked a host of eyewitnesses to genocide equally as determined and as brave as Harriet Nahanee.

Rev. Kevin Annett in his church,
Port Alberni, 1992

From a bus stop in the slums of
Vancouver, Canada

Mass Grave site, former Alberni
Indian residential school

Kevin Annett and his daughters
Elinor and Clare, 1993

Native children in Ahousaht
Village, 1993

Fig. 3a: Mortality rate records from Dr. Bryce's 1920 report

Indian Affairs. (RG 10, Volume 3957, file 140,754-1)

(Left) Evidence of fifty
percent death rate in
Canadian Indian Residential
schools, from Dr. Bryce's
government report, 1907

(Right) Newspaper account of the enormous death rate in the schools, Ottawa Citizen, November 15, 1907

(Below) Eyewitness account of a murder at United Church's Ahousaht residential school, The Vancouver Sun, December 20, 1995

(Bottom) First class action lawsuit by residential school survivors, Vancouver Sun, February 1, 1996

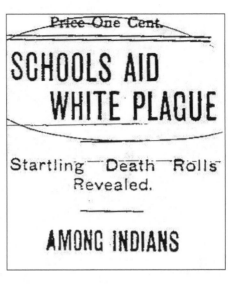

Price-One Cent.

SCHOOLS AID WHITE PLAGUE

Startling Death Rolls Revealed.

AMONG INDIANS

Beaten to death for theft of a prune

Indian elder recalls strapping of 15-year-old boy at Island residential school in 1938 by United Church minister.

MARK HUME
Vancouver Sun

A 15-year-old boy who stole a prune from a jar in the kitchen of a United Church residential school was strapped so relentlessly his kidneys failed him and he later died in bed, says a native Indian elder who was there at the time.

Archie Frank, now 68, was just 11 years old when his school mate, Albert Gray, was caught stealing in the Ahousat Residential School kitchen one night in 1938.

Frank, a retired commercial fisher, says he's never forgotten what happened to Gray, a husky youngster from the remote Vancouver Island community of Nitinat.

"He got strapped to death," said Frank in an interview on Tuesday.

"Just for stealing one prune, [Rev. A.E.] Caldwell strapped him to death.

"Beat the s—— right out of him."

Frank's story, told after a 57-year silence, crystallizes much of what the furore over residential schools is all about.

For the past year the RCMP has been probing a series of alleged abuses in church-run residential schools. So far

they have found evidence that 54 people were victims of abuse at the hands of 94 offenders. The investigation is concerned with 14 residential schools operated by the Anglican, United and Roman Catholic churches from the late 1800s to 1984.

The First United Church has come under scrutiny by the RCMP this week because of new allegations that two children were killed while at the residential school in the Port Alberni area in the 1940s and '50s.

Frank said Caldwell left Ahousat after the residential school burned down in 1940 and went on to be principal of the United Church school in Port Alberni.

Please see SCHOOL, A2

The Vancouver Sun

$1 MINIMUM OUTSIDE LOWER MAINLAND   THURSDAY, FEBRUARY 1, 1996   60 CENTS RETAIL .75 CENTS COIN BOX

15 Indian men seek millions for assaults

Rapes, beatings 30 years ago at Island residential school are the basis of a lawsuit against Ottawa, United Church.

MARK HUME
Vancouver Sun

A series of rapes and beatings that shocked a B.C. Supreme Court judge are the basis for a massive lawsuit by 15 men against the federal government, the United Church of Canada and four

administrators.

The case, filed in Vancouver on Monday, claims unspecified damages for a series of brutal, physical and sexual assaults that took place at the Port Alberni Indian Residential School during the 1960s.

Vancouver lawyer Peter Grant said that he could not put a specific dollar figure to the claim, but believes it will become the biggest suit of its kind ever filed in Canada.

"For any one of these victims the claim would be for a large amount of money. For all of them it would be massive," he

said.

"We have 15 individuals here whose lives have been destroyed."

By way of comparison, Grant said that his clients would be seeking "a lot more" than the $50 million former prime minister Brian Mulroney is seeking in a libel suit against the federal government.

"I wonder what he would have sued for if he'd lost 30 years of his life," said Grant.

"When you look at the pleadings in this case, the destruction to each of these people is immense. One of the

victims was beaten so much he became deaf. Most never finished school because of what happened to them.

They've suffered the problems of divorce, alcohol abuse, drug addiction. One described today how he can't control his bowels whenever he's under stress, because of what happened to him."

The suit follows the conviction last March of Arthur Henry Plint, who was given 11 years in jail for a series of sexual assaults that took place 30 years ago at the Alberni residential school.

Plint, who was supervisor of the boys'

dorms at the school, repeatedly abused the children in his care.

The courts heard that when some of the children complained to others, school officials, they were convinced to be silent.

When B.C. Supreme Court Justice Douglas Hogarth heard the convictions against Plint, he said he was shocked.

"I must say that I have now been in this business since 1956 as a lawyer and primarily in criminal law, and as on the bench, and I have never s—

Please see LAWSUIT, A2

Fig. 22: First lawsuits by residential school survivors, February 1, 1996

95

Nanaimo Daily News, Feb. 7, 1998

Former minister alleges officials killed students

By Nelson Bennett
Daily News

Beatings and rape weren't the only crimes committed at the Port Alberni Indian Residential School, says a former United Church minister.

Kevin Annett, who was removed from the pulpit in 1995, says at least four children at the Alberni Residential School may have died under

at the Alberni residential school, which had been run by the United Church.

"All the visits I did in native homes, they all said the same thing," Annett said. "And they said even worse. They said that kids are buried out behind the Alberni school."

"I found it incredible. But I couldn't deny what people were telling me and what I was increasingly

"I found a
16-year-old native
girl beaten to death,
with no clothes on,"

HARRY WILSON

Maisie Shaw died in 1946 after being

"I found a 16-year-old native girl beaten to death, with no clothes on."

Wilson said in a phone interview Sunday.

He said he told the principal. He was soon sent away to hospital in Nanaimo. He never did find out what happened to the girl.

Annett said the deaths have never been satisfactorily explained by either police, school or church officials, and he thinks he knows why.

Kevin Annett describes murders, The Nanaimo Daily News,
February 7, 1998

INTERNATIONAL
HUMAN RIGHTS
ASSOCIATION OF AMERICAN MINORITIES

IHRAAM

An International NGO in consultative Status (Roster) with the Economic and Social Council of the United Nations

Press Release

To: All Press and Media
Dateline: Woodinville, WA   May 25, 1998
Contact: Diana Wynne James   425-483-9251

Subject: Murder and Atrocities Subject of Tribunal

International Human Rights experts from the International Human Rights Association of American Minorities (IHRAAM) have been asked to investigate murder and atrocities at United States and Canadian Residential Schools.

The International Human Rights Association of American Minorities Northwest Regional Office serves as a Liaison for the Indigenous Peoples of the Americas and is investigating the horrific and shocking allegations by eyewitnesses who have described a legacy of torture and murder at the Canadian Indian residential schools. Following two preliminary interviews with residential school survivors at Port Alberni and Vancouver, B.C., IHRAAM is in possession of approximately seven hours of emotionally charged videotaped testimony, letters of request for help and much written documentation supporting an in-depth investigation.

Invited tribunal jurists will include respected Tribal Elders and leaders from many Indigenous Nations of the Americas and certain others drawn from the non-native community of the United States and Canada. The NorthWest International Tribunal will convene from June 12 - 14, 1998 at the Maritime Labour Centre, 1880 Triumph Street, Vancouver, B.C.

Issues to be discussed are: Forced removal from traditional lands and waters, institutional racism, physical and psychological warfare, ethnocide and murder stemming from the residential school system supported by the government of Canada and the United Church of Canada, the Catholic Church and other churches, organizations and individuals involved with the operation of the residential schools across the United States, Canada and the Northwest Territories.

Media release of U.N. agency IHRAAM concerning its
June, 1998 Tribunal into Canadian residential schools

Native kids 'used for experiments'

A church magazine says federal health tests were conducted in B.C. and Ontario residential schools in the 1940s and '50s.

SOUTHAM NEWS, VANCOUVER SUN

OTTAWA — The federal government conducted health experiments on First Nations children in residential schools in the late 1940s and early '50s, a church magazine has reported. One of the four residential schools was located in Port Alberni.

Native children were deliberately denied basic dental treatment at the United Church-run Port Alberni school and scientists also "tinkered" with the children's diets at other schools, the Anglican Journal reports.

The government did not inform many of the parents of the research the government was conducting on their children.

In a letter on Oct. 3, 1949, Dr. H.K. Brown, chief of the dental health division of the federal health department, requested staff halt some dental treatments at the Port Alberni school, the Journal reports.

"No specialized, over-all type of dental service should be provided, such as the use of sodium fluoride, dental prophylaxis or even urea compounds," he wrote in his one-page letter. "In this study dental caries and gingivitis are both important factors in assessing nutritional status."

The Anglican Journal story quotes the doctor who headed the five-year research program, now a 90-year-old nursing-home resident.

"It was not a deliberate attempt to leave children to develop caries [tooth decay] except for a limited time or place or purpose, and only then to study the effects of vitamin C or fluoride," said Dr. L.B. Pett, former chief of the nutritional division of the health department.

Pett acknowledged that "parental consent was not always obtained for those children involved in the study".

The revelation shocked George Erasmus, head of the Aboriginal Healing Foundation, which aids victims of residential-school abuse. He told the Journal the experiments were unknown to him.

The objective of the research at Indian residential school children was "to evolve methods for improving health, not only of the school children but of the whole population," Pett said in the story.

In dietary experiments, federal health officials supplied flour with added vitamins in 1949-50. Then the vitamin supplements were halted so the results could be studied.

Evidence of crimes reported at IHRAAM Tribunal, The
Vancouver Sun, April 26, 2000

Application for Admission form that
stripped legal guardianship from native
parents

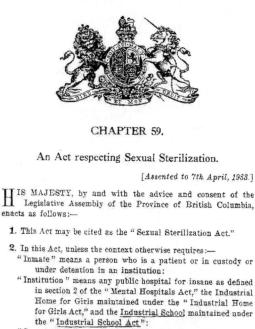

CHAPTER 59.

An Act respecting Sexual Sterilization.

[Assented to 7th April, 1933.]

HIS MAJESTY, by and with the advice and consent of the Legislative Assembly of the Province of British Columbia, enacts as follows:—

1. This Act may be cited as the "Sexual Sterilization Act."   Short title.

2. In this Act, unless the context otherwise requires:—   Interpretation.

"Inmate" means a person who is a patient or in custody or under detention in an institution:

"Institution" means any public hospital for insane as defined in section 2 of the "Mental Hospitals Act," the Industrial Home for Girls maintained under the "Industrial Home for Girls Act," and the Industrial School maintained under the "Industrial School Act":

"Superintendent," in the case of a public hospital for insane, means the Medical Superintendent of that hospital, and, in the case of the Industrial Home for Girls or the Industrial School, means the Superintendent or other head thereof.

3. For the purposes of this Act, the Lieutenant-Governor in   Board of Eug. Council may from time to time appoint three persons, one of whom shall be a Judge of a Court of Record in the Province, one of whom shall be a psychiatrist, and one of whom shall be a person experienced in social welfare work, who shall constitute a Board to be known as the "Board of Eugenics."

4. (1.) Where it appears to the Superintendent of any institution   Recommendat within the scope of this Act that any inmate of that institution, if   Superintender discharged therefrom without being subjected to an operation for sexual sterilization, would be likely to beget or bear children who

199

Sexual Sterilization Act of British Columbia, 1933, under which aboriginals were made infertile

(Top) Residential school survivors protest, Toronto, 2008

(Right) Protestors occupy Catholic church, Vancouver, 2008

Multiple grave sites at residential schools revealed

By Jim Windle
VANCOUVER

Last Thursday, during a public ceremony and press conference, conducted outside the Indian Affairs building in downtown Vancouver, Kevin Annett revealed the specific locations of 28 mass grave sites he says contains remains of children who died within the walls of residential schools across Canada.

Annett (aka Eagles Strong Voice) is spokesperson for the grassroots group known as Friends and Relatives of the Disappeared (FRD) based out of the Vancouver area. FRD is demanding that the federal government and the Catholic, Anglican and United Churches of Canada open their records and reveal the locations of all of those who died within

the system many refer to as Canada's Secret Holocaust.

The group also wants brought to justice those directly involved in murders and gross abuses against Native children within the Residential School system between the mid 1800's and 1976 when the last residential school was closed. He has uncovered evidence that points to as many a 50,000 deaths and burials in Canada's attempt to exterminate Native culture, language and customs through forced assimilation.

The world media as well as United Nations agencies received the release Thursday although most of the mainstream news outlets seemed to ignore the revelation. Along with the released burial locations, was the announcement of the newly formed

continued to page 5

April 11, 2008   MetroNews Vancouver

Alleged mass graves listed

By KRISTEN THOMPSON
Metro Vancouver

Members of a group that claims there are mass graves of residential school children released a list of alleged graves yesterday and demanded an independent inquiry.

Kevin Annett of Friends and Relatives of the Disappeared says thousands of children are buried in 28 mass graves across Canada, and that his group is taking its list to the United Nations. The list includes Port Alberni, Alert Bay and Mission, but so far there's no proof of the graves.

"We're calling for an in-

Greene

quiry because we don't think the government or church that ran these schools are the ones to be investigating them."

Sylvester Greene, who went to the United Church residential school in Edmonton, said he was hired by his abusive minister to bury a five-year-old Inuit boy in an unmarked grave.

"This really hurts to talk about," he said, breaking down in tears. "At 64 years old, it still hurts to talk about."

Mass Graves identified near former Indian residential schools, Teka News, 2008

The Unending Vigil

22
Interlude – The Children's War

When the LORD your God brings you into the land you are entering to possess and drives out before you many nations ... and you have defeated them, then you must destroy them totally. Make no treaty with them, and show them no mercy. ... This is what you are to do to them: Break down their altars, smash their sacred stones, cut down their [trees] and burn [them] in the fire. For you are a people holy to the LORD your God. The LORD your God has chosen you out of all the peoples on the face of the earth.
Deuteronomy 7:1–2, 5–6, NIV

No word can ever match the horror of what went on behind those stone walls. For the terrible uniqueness of the residential schools genocide in Canada was that it was aimed at children. Search our bloody world history, and one is challenged to find a plan calculated to destroy primarily the children of entire nations. Even the Nazi Holocaust was not so intentionally focused.

One of the few historical parallels to what happened in Canada occurred in the practice of Byzantine emperors, who routinely ordered that the infants of conquered foreign kings be abducted, reared in Byzantine culture and their imperial protocol, and then, as re-programmed adults in service to the Empire, sent back among their former countrymen as satraps and colonial rulers.

There, and here, the practices, while not identical, achieved the same result. The plan worked, extremely well.

'Aboriginal' means, literally, 'not of the original group': an abnormality foisted on entire peoples across the globe by their largely European conquerors, who simply exterminated most of them and then repatterned the survivors into a permanent and landless underclass. Queen Elizabeth I tried to 'aboriginalize' the Irish in the sixteenth century, but it wouldn't 'take' among such a rebellious people. It eventually succeeded to a greater degree in Scotland, and most other places the English Crown devastated, including Canada.

In summarizing this philosophy of Empire, British General Maitland commented, in 1839, that English rule over 'savages' amounted to 'a good thrashing followed by great kindness'. While hardly kind, English and French rule over the Indian nations of Canada was at least conceptualized as such by the conquerors, and is still faithfully felt and taught to be so.

Predictably, this 'kind' genocide in Canada was led by the Christian churches, brought into being, legalized and protected by the Crown and the Vatican. And they succeeded far beyond their wildest hopes, for a simple reason: the genocidal method in Canada was fashioned by the Jesuits, who were adept at brainwashing young children, and who did so under a secret oath that allowed them license to subvert, kill and torture any non-Catholics and their communities in the defense of the Roman Church and the Pope.

'Give me a child for seven years and he will be ours for life,' bragged Jesuit founder Ignatius Loyola. He did not exaggerate.

Jesuit-trained Bishop Paul Durieu designed the Canadian Indian residential school system during the 1880s. Its method was simple and brutal: to destroy the traditional leaders of a targeted native nation, supplant them with Catholicized Indian 'chiefs', usually brought in from other regions, and then kidnap and isolate the children of the traditional leaders so that the continuity of indigenous tradition would be broken forever.

'Once the heathens have forgotten their barbarous ways,' outlined Durieu in a letter to the Vatican in 1886, 'and once their children are free of their parents' corrupting influence, they can be used at our leisure.'

Durieu's idea caught on, and the Protestant churches, not wanting to be left out of the action, soon adopted his model, and broadened it to sweep in all the Indian children of any given area. The Canadian government sanctioned the entire strategic plan in November 1910 at a closed meeting in Ottawa with all the churches present: a sort of Canadian Wannsee Protocol.

The specific method of Durieu's system was massive terror and trauma aimed at generations of children, with the result that memory, allegiance and identity would be 'wiped as clean as a slate', to quote one church official.

The man forgot to add that, in the process, a lot of the little slates would get shattered and destroyed.

Rian Malan, a South African writer, in his struggle to understand the identity of his Boer people, observed that 'We cannot come to terms with what we don't understand.' And colonizers like Euro-Canadians can never understand themselves, let alone the ones they've conquered, simply because their culture is predicated on a vast system of lies, which overlay one vast killing field.

23
January 1996 – Vancouver, Canada

The first weeks of the year that would see me lose my children and my livelihood were like a free-fire zone, as the church and its minions hit me from all sides at once. At the very moment when they were staging the divorce with my ex-wife and engineering the loss of my children, the United Church began the final process of expelling me from the church.

Larger forces were prompting this barrage against me. On February 1, 1996, the United Church was named as the primary defendant in the first native class action lawsuit in Canadian history. It was brought by fifteen survivors of their Alberni residential school, many of whom I had worked with.

Two days later, church officials decided to defrock me for good, simultaneous with their assisting Anne with her divorce.

After Anne's Christmas Eve announcement that she was leaving me, she disappeared one night with both of my daughters, and for days, panic stricken, I had no idea where they were. But the morning after that first sleepless night, I was summoned by a knock on our door in UBC student housing, and was presented with divorce and custody papers by a smirking young process server.

Knowing of the looming residential school lawsuits, and my role in aiding the plaintiffs, the church clearly had decided to finish me off, as brutally and as quickly as possible: something they even admitted at my subsequent 'defrocking' trial.

But on that first day of life without my children, there was only agony. I remember sinking to the floor of our tiny apartment, sobbing, as I leafed through the papers served on me, and stared, dumbstruck, at affidavits from in-laws and friends whom I had loved, which castigated me as an unfit person and terrible father. I stared in utter disbelief at pages from my personal journal that Anne had stolen and photocopied, and submitted as 'proof' that I was 'mentally unstable'.

The court papers demanded full custody of Clare and Elinor, minimal visitation rights for me, and most of our family assets. Anne, and her church allies, were going for the jugular.

Family court was an unmitigated nightmare that allowed me to see the sadistic and hopelessly corrupt nature of Canada's judicial system. The purpose of the courtroom pretense was akin to my professional 'defrocking' later in that year: to criminalize and publicly destroy an 'inconvenient' man. And every level of society seemed to gather for the kill.

For instance, during the very week when the judge in our divorce case was deciding who would have custody of our children, Brian Thorpe contrived with his journalist friend Douglas Todd to publish an article in the *Vancouver Sun*, which claimed that I was suffering from a 'psychiatric disturbance'. Anne's lawyer then met with Phil Spencer, my seminary friend who had signed my dismissal letter, and obtained confidential church documents that he was able to produce in court, establishing that the church considered me a nutcase.

Far be it from a busy divorce court judge to question such ecclesiastical schemes. The custody decision concerning Clare and Elinor went in favor of Anne in the time it takes to drop a gavel. Suddenly, I was limited to seeing my daughters for eight hours a week, and I was ordered out of our family home.

It suddenly felt that my heart and guts had been torn from me, and every day became a nightmare of pain. But I kept myself together for Clare and Elinor, who were still only seven and four years old. They had enough anxieties of their own to deal with, especially since they knew that their mother had already taken up with another man, Brian Arkell, and she had told both Clare and Elinor not to tell me about him.

Parenthetically, as to Anne's divorce suit, I was to learn later,

the United Church picked up the tab: $50,000, give or take –
enough to run my doomed food bank, which that same church
had scuttled as financially too expensive, for twenty years.

There followed the lowest period of my life, just as I was
turning forty. How I lived through that time is a continuing
mystery to me. But with each new assault, something was
emerging in me that I could never have imagined. Strength,
somehow unaffected by suffering, or even events, but arising
from somewhere else.

It seems that when you are reduced to nothing you begin
seeing with absolute clarity, and you gain a new capacity to act
without fear of consequence, because nothing remains for you to
lose. This inner transformation may be what Desmond Tutu said
about the incarceration and ultimate triumph of Nelson Mandela:

'When he went to prison he was just an angry young man. His
prison made him bigger.'

My own suffering was all for another purpose, but I was only
to learn this as it unfolded.

With the commencement of the first residential school lawsuit
against the government and the United Church in February of
1996, the newspapers were filled with the desperate protestations
of church officials that it was the government that had been
responsible for what had happened to all those residential school
children. The government, in turn, blamed the churches, but in a
bland fashion, without suggesting retributive justice of any kind.
But what I had begun to uncover in those dusty microfilm spools
in the Koerner Library irrevocably disproved the church's efforts
to evade responsibility for its crimes.

The fact was, this truth had to move from dusty spools to
public knowledge. Bruce Gunn had said to me, long before my
final expulsion from the church, 'This is just like something out
of a Kafka novel. None of it makes any sense.'

On the contrary, I was able to realize even then that it all made
perfect sense. For thus do guilty parties act. And I had it in my

hands, even amidst my collapsing life, to lay the blame where it was due.

Harriet Nahanee had invited me to her home on the Squamish reserve shortly after I met her at our December protest where she had told the press of Maisie Shaw's murder. In her gruff manner, she flatly told me that I wasn't to give up. It's at that point that she invited me to make a more public stand for her people, and for all the lost children.

'We don't need healing,' she said. 'We aren't the problem: they are.'

I leaped at this chance to ratchet up the struggle. The times demanded it. For as a result of the first lawsuit against the church, within the following year, thousands of legal actions would be brought by survivors against all the churches. Drawing on my microfilms discovery at UBC, I began assisting the survivors and their lawyers with documents that confirmed everything, and more, that they were claiming about their torture in the residential schools.

Harriet began to bring me to several of the first healing circles among school survivors, mostly along the skid row strip of the downtown east side of Vancouver, where thousands of native people still struggle to survive. I was familiar with the neighborhood, having done my internship at First United Church along the worst slum concourse in the city. Among the native people of those streets, my expulsion from the United Church seemed to win me instant credibility and acceptance by them, as fellow victims of the same church.

Almost at once, the survivors asked me to record their verbal recollections, establish and document their stories in writing, and help them to gain public support for what seemed to be the ultimate David and Goliath confrontation.

Previously, I had attended a few healing circles in Port Alberni, but they had been tepid affairs compared to what I now experienced in the Vancouver native world.

Most Indians in Canada live off reservations, often in the larger urban centers, where they struggle at a standard of living ranked 64th in the world, below that of Thailand. Theirs is worse than third-world-nation status, certainly more apparent and jarring because it exists within and in plain view of an affluent society.

In Vancouver, these urban aboriginals are denied the benefits, however diluted, that are accorded their reserve counterparts and their chiefs and band councils, who receive the perhaps guilt-ridden largesse of the federal government.

What I immediately learned from Harriet Nahanee was that these off-reserve Indians, at least on the west coast, are the descendants, the surviving residue, of many of the children of the residential schools. They became by default my new congregation, and my best supporters.

The people with whom I came in direct contact lived, or tried to live, among the squalid rooming houses and fleabag hotels of East Hastings Street. This was the soil from which the movement Harriet Nahanee and I planted sprouted and grew, all during 1996 and 1997. That movement was the seed from which all events since then have grown, not the least of which was the Prime Minister's limp 'apology' to survivors made in Parliament in June of 2008.

The natives of East Hastings Street are a people totally ignored by their own leaders, the official native organizations, which are dependent on government support and therefore reluctant to back any issue not on the government's agenda. In fact, the 'establishment Indian organizations', far from being of any help to our cause were, as we proceeded, in direct confrontation with us.

It was a stormy but breathtaking time for me, as I enthusiastically accepted the role of becoming their advocate. From the gut-wrenching and often horrifying sessions where now-grown men and women described their torture and mutilation in residential school settings, I would hasten back to the UBC library archives and there, among the undisputed records of the Canadian establishment, uncover documents, letters and reports that proved everything these unlettered survivors were describing with such agony.

I shared many of these documents with the healing circle participants. I showed them a copy of the Application for Admission form, which forced their parents to surrender them to the residential schools. I told them how their long anger at their mothers and fathers for not getting them out of those hell-holes was misplaced, since this one form had robbed them of their legal guardianship rights and placed that in the hands of the residential school principals.

None of them had known this. They were ignorant of the fact that a Canadian law and an official document had been the cause of their lifelong misery, not their parents. Some of them burst into tears at this revelation; others stood, dumbstruck. It was as if a dense cloud was lifted from them. And only then they could begin to disclose, and name names, and take action.

I was struck that day with the realization that my work could now have an even better and more direct impact on the lives of residential school survivors than before. Despite the way in which the very unearthing of the truth of what had happened to them terrified many survivors, they now had the weapon of knowledge, and more and more, that began to empower them and cause them to speak out.

As I saw the wall of fear and silence begin to crumble, I realized that what I was going through among these unexpected people was more than a personal vindication. In a concrete way I was able to feel that I was rediscovering a meaningful purpose in my own life, just at the time when the church was trying to destroy it. Working with these people literally kept me alive, as did my rare but joyous moments with my daughters.

And yet the pain that accompanied all this was almost too

much to bear. My personal losses, the dislocation in my own life, were magnified somehow by the continuing nightmare of what my own people and culture had done to entire nations. The force of this realization jarred me loose forever from any desire to seek readmission into the mainstream comforts of my culture.

After decades of sporadically claiming to be a 'radical', I was finally involved in actual dissent that really mattered, since it could get me killed. My former gestures of rebellion had been largely intellectual, leaving me free to go on living concurrently within the status quo. But now, with a sudden shock, my own trauma following my expulsion from the church, the loss of my family and any livelihood, had somehow detached me from the comfortable and complicit traditions of western civilization.

Ever since that time of change, that shock has caused in me a constant sense of dislocation, of being adrift in history without any strong familiar moorings. All of the old answers and identifications have withered and died in me. But for too long afterward, I continued to dwell on their demise rather than on what was being made possible by their departure.

Later, my world would assume more clarity, as when dust settles, and in place of what I at first regretted losing, I would welcome an incredible new birth, a view of my real place, which I owe to the changes that began when strangers showed me a new world.

Undoubtedly because of my heightened activism and public profile, by my refusal to be crushed by their attacks, the church became all the more committed to my destruction during 1996, the year that they finally defrocked me.

The reason was obvious. I could imagine hordes of litigating Indians haunting the nightmares of United Church officials and their lawyers. And while in February of that year, two days after residential school survivors began suing them, the handful of men who had arranged my firing finally decided to publicly 'defrock' me as a minister, it wasn't until August that that particular farce began to unfold.

In part, that was because I had not cooperated in my own execution, continuing to demand why I had been fired and what the charges were against me. This threw them into confusion, naturally, since what they had to indicate as my offense was solely that I had drawn attention to the church's own wrong-doing. Since that couldn't be acknowledged, a new scenario had to be fabricated, to make me appear 'unbalanced' and a habitual malcontent.

To be beaten up by lawyers and public relations specialists is somewhat like being worked over by trained thugs who leave no visible marks. To be the subject of outrageous stories, to be publicly portrayed as unstable and rancorous, and especially to experience friends, and sometimes even family members, turn away from you because of that public portrayal – all of this is a crucifixion of the spirit from which it is well-nigh impossible to recover.

This, I came to realize, is the ultimate method for dealing with insurgency, and since I was indeed a terrorist in the eyes of the church establishment, they engaged their long history as counter-insurgency experts, which they had honed since the Inquisition. The genius of counter-insurgency lies not in directly combating the insurgent, but rather in brainwashing the public and by inference the media, which then turn on the rebel, rendering him unrecognized, irrelevant and in fact invisible.

How any corporation, including the church, deals with dissi-dents I sum up in what I call the Formula of the Three 'D's': Deny, Distract, and Discredit. In my case, this meant that the church officials denied the real reasons for my firing, distracted the public with a red-herring version of me and my work, and discredited me in the eyes of anyone who might come to my aid.

It wasn't enough that the United Church had thrown me out of my job and vocation, destroyed years of devoted work in the Alberni valley, and gutted the hopes and the lives of hundreds of poor aboriginal people who had come into my church. Nor was it enough that they had deliberately broken up my family, and later bankrolled the removal of my children from me. The church insisted on my public humiliation, on my public display in the stocks, if you like, where I could be pelted and covered with disdain.

But as Walt Whitman once lyrically observed, 'Do we think victory great? So it is – but now it seems to me, when it cannot be helped, that defeat is great, and that death and dismay are great.'

The church's placing me in the public stocks in fact had the opposite effect to what they intended. For from there, I was suddenly elevated to a platform from which the world could see me and the forces, and witnesses, swirling about me.

The life and death of my ancestor Peter Annet struck home to me, then, as never before: an aging humanist scholar and pamphleteer in England, who in 1769 had offended the Church of England with his 'seditious' questioning of the Bible and church authority, and as a result had been imprisoned and placed in the stocks outside London's Newgate Prison. But Peter, like me, had left his mark on time and space all that more because of his calvary.

The time had come for all the stocks to be thrown open, and the prisoners set free. But how, exactly?

24
1997 – Vancouver, Canada

As divorce, sabotage and defrocking assault the man, he comes all that closer to those for whom he was destined.

Throughout the months of his delisting hearing at the hands of the BC Conference at St John's United Church, Harriet Nahanee had been a constant presence outside the church, where she walked to and fro adorned with a simple handmade sign, declaring, '504 Years of Genocide: Where is Justice in the United Church?'

Harriet was there each time Jon Jessiman and Brian Thorpe entered, scurrying past her with bowed heads as though she was a panhandler, to get into the church where the inquisition was proceeding. Never once did they bother responding to her sign, or to her simple words, 'I saw Maisie Shaw get killed in your residential school.' But she never stopped her vigil.

Whenever the droning indictment within reached increasingly outlandish proportions, Kevin Annett would look out the window and see Harriet pacing in her lone protest, her placard proclaiming the essential question. And he would carry on another day.

The day Bruce Gunn and Kevin Annett walked out of the kangaroo court called a 'church hearing', Harriet was there to greet them. Oceans of culture and experience separated the aging woman from the two men, but in her drawn and tired face they could see her understanding of what was going on with the young clergyman.

'You might think they'll get away with this, Kevin, but they won't,' Harriet said quietly to him. 'I've had to wait fifty years for justice.

Maybe you will, too. But you can't ever give up. Too many people are depending on you.'

As if to illustrate her words, during the summer of 1997, after Kevin's defrocking, Harriet suggested to him that they form a group called the Circle of Justice. It was a movement that aimed to bring to international justice the churches responsible for the residential school massacres.

Harriet and Kevin began organizing the residential school survivors in earnest during the autumn of 1997, in weekly forums and healing circles in the downtown east side of Vancouver. Nothing like this had ever happened before in Canada. Not only were the gatherings unique, but so too was the message of the Circle: namely, that the system that planned and committed the crime will never bring healing, or justice. Only the survivors, and allies at home and abroad, will win these things.

This perspective, of course, placed Harriet, Kevin and their small guerilla band in a direct collision course with the 'official' native politicians placed in affluence by the system that spawned the crime. The self-appointed 'chiefs' of the national 'Assembly of First Nations' – Harriet liked to say that 'AFN' stood for the 'Around the Fort Natives' – had concluded that there was no money to be made talking about murder, sterilization and pedophilia in residential schools, particularly when the same native politicians had been implicated in many instances in these crimes. But with the appearance of juicy personal injury lawsuits dangling before every aboriginal nation across the country, the establishment Indians came out of the woodwork right when the Circle began to form and make a public stink.

By the time the Circle of Justice's work eventually spawned the more prominent United Nations' IHRAAM Tribunal, in the summer of 1998, the politically motivated chiefs were working overtime to sabotage the Circle – which they eventually did – and drive both Harriet and Kevin into obscurity.

For it was in the Circle's gatherings that the world began to learn from ravaged men and women the full horror of the residential school death camps, and the human toll they had taken.

The magnitude was matched only by the degree of the atrocities, and both were unconscionable: children tortured with electricity, whipped and starved to death, beaten, humiliated and gang raped, and even farmed out to wealthy johns through police-protected pedophile rings – horrors that had been known to the public before, but always taking place in other remote places such as India or Bangladesh or Southeast Asia. But in Canada?

The list of atrocities was verified in records and documents Kevin had begun to discover and publish as part of his doctoral research at the University of British Columbia. This was no wild conjecture, no fabricated native gossip or hearsay, as the churches and government continued to suggest. The establishment itself was their chief witness.

It was small wonder that United Church officials scuttled Kevin's program at UBC when they did, right at the same time that they were 'defrocking' and publicly excommunicating him during 1996 and 1997, and helping destroy his family. The church could no more have allowed Kevin the legitimacy and respectability of a doctoral degree than it could allow him to continue to preach from a pulpit.

He and those survivors were becoming a formidable combination: something that became more apparent as 1998 dawned, and the Circle of Justice began to hold public forums demanding that the churches and government be brought to trial for the residential school atrocities.

The vacuum of leadership among the native bands at that time became increasingly apparent, because of the system of directing all money to the band councils and chiefs, who often lived in baronial luxury, while the people received marginal benefit, if any. Failed even more were the off-reservation native people, who had migrated to the cities by default.

Ironically, this total lack of leadership worked to the advantage of Harriet and Kevin, and their unpaid efforts. Because most native people, and especially most residential school survivors, had no leadership that would actually fight for them, the people came forward eagerly in response to the Circle, and Harriet and Kevin. And it was this response that prompted them in early 1998 to shift gears, escalating the Circle beyond merely serving as a 'healing' program to one of waging direct combat with church and state.

To do so, it was imperative that they move their fulcrum beyond the colonial jurisdiction of Canada altogether. They began to plan to convene the first International Tribunal into the genocide called 'Christian Canada'.

25
February 1998 – East Side, Vancouver, Canada

You're a good Anglican, Ed. You need to have lots of children. I only
sterilize the pagans.
Dr George Darby Sr,
United Church missionary doctor,
to Ed Martin of the Heiltsuk Nation,
Bella Bella, BC, June 1952

'This stuff is a matter for international law,' Diana James said to
me, after her first interviews with witnesses from residential
schools. Diana and her husband Rudy were in Vancouver representing IHRAAM, a United Nations human rights agency, after
being invited by me and Harriet Nahanee.

'These are crimes against humanity, not "personal injuries".
Why is no one talking about that?'

'Why, indeed,' I replied.

'How long has this been going on?' asked Rudy James. He
looks at Harriet Nahanee, standing quietly beside me.

'Oh, I'd say about 150 years.'

'Well,' Rudy James said, 'we're going to recommend that the
IHRAAM hold a Tribunal here in Vancouver, and we won't
postpone it. We'll try to do so by June.'

26
April 1987 – Chiapas, Southern Mexico
Interlude

In the spring of that year, while still a seminary student in Vancouver, Kevin Annett becomes aware that he knows more about events thousands of miles away than those two blocks down the road. He begins to work with aboriginals on East Hastings Street in Vancouver as part of his work at First United Church, but he really knows nothing about who they are and what they have suffered at the hands of his own people.

So it is curious how, just at that time, he is asked to take part in a 'fact-finding tour', sponsored by a church 'outreach' group, to the Mayan refugee camps of southern Mexico.

The brutal reality he witnesses in these camps begins to convince him that he can do nothing, really, for Guatemalan Indians – he cannot even speak their language and has no intention of staying among them. He feels completely inadequate and ridiculous in southern Mexico – a comfortable progressive who has a plane ticket back to Canada.

But something in the lives and the spirit of the Mayan refugees awakens in him an urge and need to go out among the aboriginal people of his own country in something beyond a token or self-serving manner.

He feels none of this when he arrives in Mexico. Somehow surviving the hell and air pollution of Mexico City, he finds himself with five other Canadians in the jungles of Chiapas, breathing a damp air that is primeval and completely alive. They ramble over dusty mountain roads and up snowy peaks in a bus that keeps breaking down, until they come out onto the southern plain bordering Guatemala: a hot and dry semi-desert that soon begins frying away all his assumptions. After several days, they arrive at the Nueva Esperanza refugee camp, housing over 3,000 people.

In spite of its name, he sees no hope at all, at first. Their guide is a defrocked former Catholic priest named Fidel, who has been thrown out of the church for antagonizing the local landowners with his sermons calling for better wages for their field workers. He spends his days now serving the refugees as their priest and bringing in foreign fact-finding missions.

There is a very large price on Fidel's head, and predictably, two years later, he is shot to death by one of the landowners' gunmen. He is a simple, pure-hearted man, and in a way yet to be revealed he is charting a path for the young Canadian who meets him.

He smiles from behind his thick beard as the Canadians approach the refugee camp, in response to a comment that they hope to do some good for the refugees.

'You can't,' he says, through an interpreter. 'Stop thinking you can and you may learn something here.'
His words at first offend the visitors, but they see quickly the truth of his statement. Fidel helps to prepare them.

'This part of Mexico produces more hydro-electricity than any part of the country but none of my people have electric power. We produce more corn than other states but the children here are all starving. The system murders the Indians like it has always done, and for the same reason: to get their land and make money.'
Their bus pulls up at the end of a dirt road and they alight. A few small children stare out at them through the cracks of bamboo shacks and from behind tottering fences. They hide when they see the strangers, but Fidel gestures to them and says,
'Their parents were killed by the Guatemalan army. Some of them saw

their mothers and fathers hacked to death with machetes. We try to keep them alive but the problem is more than a lack of food. Even though diseases kill more than a hundred children every month here, that's not the real problem. All of these kids are dying from the inside out, of a heart illness. Without a purpose, without their own language and culture, they will all die off: maybe here, maybe in the cities.'

Women and men begin drifting toward them cautiously, and when they see Fidel they break into smiles and begin talking away in Quiche and Mam, their indigenous languages. Another guy shows up and begins translating into Spanish for them. Even the kids begin opening up to them, and one little boy keeps staring at Kevin with huge, watery brown eyes, his belly swollen, completely naked, the hordes of flies sticking to him as he stands unashamed and curious. He follows them everywhere as they are led about the camp.

The refugees' pride and joy is the little one-room schoolhouse where they try to teach their surviving children the Indian languages and culture. There are no notebooks, no pencils, not even a blackboard in the school room, only a bare dirt floor. But here something stronger than death is trying to find new life in children barely able to stand.

'What we need isn't money,' explains one of the village elders, an older woman. 'That will not bring us back our land or our heart. Our leaders are the poorest among us because they serve the people all day and forget about themselves. They know like we all do that we will survive or die together.

'Our future is in our children, and how well they remember who they are and why our Creator has put us here. If they forget this, they have no future.'

As if to demonstrate what she meant, the elder leads the foreigners to another sugar cane shack where food is spread out on a ramshackle table: mostly tortillas and black beans. Kevin assumes that the famished children will be fed first, but the visitors are asked to sit down in front of the food. They are the honored guests, and they are to eat first.

Kevin looks at the horde of hungry children who stand outside, and he automatically lifts his plate and begins to take it to them. But Fidel holds his arm firmly and shakes his head. His touch says everything, and he, Kevin, sits down with the other fat North Americans in front of the food that is all the refugees have to eat.

Then Kevin notices something even more shocking: on the edge of each of their plates is a small pile of scrambled eggs. He has seen maybe one or two scrawny chickens in the entire camp.

Fidel is watching carefully, as if he is conducting some sort of test. Perhaps sensing his thoughts, Fidel nods and says,
'Those are the only eggs the refugees have. It's their tradition to give their best to strangers.'
Kevin keeps staring at the food and, seeing the many eyes on him, he lifts the fork and eats their eggs and beans, knowing there will be nothing left for the children.

'We live at their expense, every day,' he writes later, and as a rich North American he does not want to face that violent truth, but there it is, acting itself out in a small and unnoticed place.

But something else is happening there, too: a conversion of sorts within him. A change that was meant to be.

Fidel knows what is happening; it seems to please him no end. After their meal, they are led into a small, ramshackle church where mass is held for the refugees every day. People begin to pray. Fidel is smiling like a Cheshire cat, filled with the same simple joy and belonging that is in the eyes of every single refugee, including the dying and stumbling children. A simple joy and belonging.

Kevin stares at the wooden cross and the poor peasant impaled on it, and a clarity beyond description floods over him. Even though the way of the world leads to this suffering, the final word lies only and completely in love: but not as it is in North America, in gestures that make the fat and the guilty feel comfortable.

The love Kevin senses among these refugees make him feel poorer than they – much poorer. For where in his world do people work and die for each other? Who among the churchgoers and 'radicals' he knows in Vancouver would work for nothing and expend themselves night and day for their neighbors?

The self-sacrifice of the Mayan refugees is natural, not learned. Their love flows from them like a waterfall over a thankful and thirsty land, bringing life to everyone. It was surely once there for everyone, even among his people. But some terrible thing has dried up that natural wellspring, so that they hunger now for that which no thing can provide.

Kevin's sense is that he is the starving one, not these refugees. And he has been brought down to sit at the feet of these noble, true people of God.

Jesus' words about the first being last, about the hungry being blessed, have meaning for the first time in his life, among these strangers. The miracle is true, but it has nothing to do with words, or rituals, or even Christianity.

Away from these people, he knows that he will never again taste such pure and functioning love, such a real community, where all are cared for and honored. Knowing he must go, he despairs at the thought of returning home.

His doomed but joyous friend Fidel must know of his angst, for his deep-brown eyes stay on him for much of the trip back to San Cristobal. He jokes with them about how he was defrocked by the church for being converted to Christianity by the Indians.

Years later, when Kevin has suffered precisely the same fate, for the same reason, he knows that Fidel's words were meant for him. Fidel knows that he is training for the ministry, and sees the choice he too will have to make one day, between Christ and the church.

As they part, Fidel takes Kevin's arm and says to him,

'Whenever you are in doubt, go to the hungriest child you know and ask him what to do.'

27
June 12, 1998 – East Side, Vancouver, Canada

A Nanaimo aboriginal man, Bill Seward, describes seeing his six-year-old sister Maggie thrown out of a window to her death by a nun at the Kuper Island residential school.

'We weren't allowed to see a lawyer or nothing,' says Seward. 'The Mounties threatened to kill us if we ever told anything. The whole thing was just covered up.'

A Vancouver Island woman of the Cowichan Nation, Sarah Modeste, tells of being sterilized against her will by a Dr James Goodbrand in Duncan, BC in the spring of 1953.

'He said because I married Freddie, a traditional chief, I'd have to have an operation. I tried to get away but the Mounties brought me to him. I could never have another child after that. Goodbrand did that to lots of our women. He told me later that he was being paid $300 by Indian Affairs for every native woman he sterilized.'

Sarah and Bill and dozens of other survivors of a massacre are grouped in front of a panel of men and women, most of whom are aboriginals. The hall is sparsely filled with people, but no reporters are present, even though all of the media had been invited to the event. Elders stand ready with eagle feathers and sweetgrass and sage to smudge the storytellers, and help them through their agony as they struggle to recollect.

It is the opening session of the historic first International Tribunal into Canadian Indian residential schools. Twelve judges and three United Nations observers are present. With them is Kevin Annett.

Stories of atrocities from the witnesses that day are not limited to the past. Six different people describe present-day pedophile and drug-trafficking rings being run by government-funded native chiefs in northern British Columbia. The same chiefs have also signed secret deals with resource companies like Alcan and the North American Water and Power Alliance, and forced their own people off their land.

Kevin Annett tells the Tribunal:

> *'There is written evidence that shows that the RCMP and its officers were deputized in the 1930s, and perhaps even earlier, as truant officers for the residential schools. They literally dragged kids away from their parents and delivered them to the custody of the residential schools, such as the one in Port Alberni. They'd be the ones to hunt down runaways. Often they'd bury the children killed in the schools, and would issue fake death certificates. The same kind of assaults by the Mounties against native people continues with impunity today. The RCMP can't impartially investigate reports of murder in the residential schools, because their own agency is implicated in the crimes.'*

For three days, nearly a hundred survivors of the church residential schools describe on record every offense defined as genocide by the United Nations Convention of that name in a declaration passed in 1948, and ratified by the Government of Canada in 1952.

The task of the Tribunal is to interrogate the eyewitnesses, record their stories, and submit both a report and recommendations to IHRAAM and the United Nations. The recommendations will include the question of whether Canada and its churches are guilty of what have been declared to be crimes against humanity.

Rudy James, representing the IHRAAM, is chairman of the Tribunal. He is a Tlingit native from Alaska, a man in his late fifties. Acting as Tribunal judges are a dozen aboriginal elders from nine nations across

North America. Kevin Annett serves as the official recorder, archivist and research assistant at the event.

Off the record, on the second day of the proceedings, Rudy James, in a private conversation with Kevin Annett, declares: 'We're on our way to bringing Canada and its churches to another Nuremburg trial.'
There is scant reason to accuse Rudy James of exaggeration. A group of survivors from the Catholic residential school on Kuper Island, British Columbia, arrive on the second day and describe in considerable detail how children were flogged, injected with experimental drugs and sometimes died as a result, having been brutalized in isolation chambers by 'German-speaking doctors' during 1939, and again during the late 1940s.

Other witnesses' voices are heard in abundance, pouring forth day after day. Many of them are older people now, but their voices break with emotion.

'I don't know why they hated me so much, when I was just a little girl,' says one woman from Vancouver Island. 'They shoved a needle through my tongue when I was eight years old. They killed young girls who the priests got pregnant, and buried them in secret south of the Kuper Island school.'
'They made us keep quiet,' says an elderly native from Chemainus. 'First the priest and the Mounties, and then our own chiefs told us never to talk about our friends who were killed at the school. The priests invented fake stories of how the kids "committed suicide".

'My name is Archie Frank,' came the voice of another witness. 'I'm an Ahousaht elder and I was at the Alberni school in 1938. I seen the principal at the school, Mr Caldwell, beat an Indian kid named Albert Gray to death. They caught Albert stealing a prune and Caldwell he strapped him to death. Beat the shit right out of him.'

By the second day of the IHRAAM Tribunal, with growing courage, there is more talk of modern-day atrocities, in addition to past crimes. A Squamish woman stands up.

'I was told by my chief and band council that I'd never get funding for my college course if I spoke at the Tribunal today. They've been telling everybody on the reserve not to talk about what they know about the murders and sterilization stuff.'
Asked by a tribunal judge why the native leaders would suppress the truth about the residential schools, the woman answers:

'Because the chiefs are all child molesters themselves. They've been that way since they were informers for the priests at the residential schools.'
A man and wife from the Carrier Nation in northern BC describe their attempts to expose a pedophile ring in the Moricetown area.

'Every time we talk about it, we get arrested by the Mounties. Once we were beaten up by guys sent around by the Carrier-Sekani chiefs.'

When stories implicating native chiefs in drug dealing and child trafficking begin to surface at the Tribunal, abrupt changes start happening. It first begins to be evident in the sudden unwillingness of witnesses to speak. It is as though a shadow has descended over the Tribunal. Some people even begin to leave.

28
June 14, 1998 – The Third Day

If we investigated every death of an Indian child in a residential
school we'd be at it for years.
Sgt Gerry Peters, Royal Canadian Mounted Police, 'E'
Division, Vancouver, BC, July 3, 1997, in conversation

I had been too involved in my work at the Tribunal, recording the
stories and preparing the witnesses to notice what was going on
at first. But by the third day, I was forcefully made aware of a new
tone in the proceedings in the person of Dean Wilson, a large
native man who I knew to be in the employ, and attending at the
behest of, a prominent chief by the name of Ed John. There had
already been incriminating testimony concerning Chief Ed John
shared by some of the witnesses.

Dean Wilson cornered me in the hall outside the Tribunal
early in the morning of the third day, and shoved me against a
wall.

'You'd better cut out this shit right now!' he yelled at me. One
beefy hand came up to seize my neck, forcing my head against
the wall. 'We're the ones who speak for the residential school
victims, get it?'

'No,' I said, glaring back at him. 'I don't get it.'

He increased the pressure. 'Eddy John ain't going to take this
shit lying down. You better know that. And you better back off
right now!'

Wilson gave me a final shove, and then turned and walked
away.

I was amazed at the openness with which Wilson was
divulging the name of his boss. Chief Ed John was one of the
most powerful Indian politicians in Canada, a government

insider and millionaire, the head of the collaborationist 'First Nations Summit', and one of the men being named as a criminal that very day by Tribunal eyewitnesses.

It was the first inkling of a campaign of sabotage that began to unravel the successes that we had begun to score.

Apart from Wilson's muscular warning, the sabotage wasn't that obvious, at first. It came, instead, in the form of innuendo and gossip spread by an individual named Jim Craven, an actual judge at the Tribunal who had appeared out of nowhere to volunteer his services. Craven was gossiping to the other judges that Rudy James, the Tribunal organizer and chief IHRAAM delegate, was sleeping with some of the eyewitness. Craven also claimed that I was a crazy eccentric who had paid natives to make up stories, and that I was trying to 'recruit' natives into my church: an interesting idea, since I had no church.

Jim Craven, who looked as white as me, had presented himself at the Tribunal on its first day as a volunteer judge and a member of the Blackfoot Nation. I didn't know at the time that Craven had been denounced by the Sea Shepherd Society and the American Indian Movement some years before as a spy and agent provocateur. Eventually, he would be the one largely responsible for scuttling the Tribunal by convincing the IHRAAM board that Rudy James had falsified its findings.

Suddenly, after two days of testimony and highly charged drama in the union hall where we met, eyewitnesses simply stopped coming to the microphone. Many more people began to leave the hall without explanation. Two of the judges who had been most cooperative, Royce and Lydia White Calf from the Oglala Lakota Nation, were harassed and later followed by men in an unmarked van.

On the final day of the Tribunal, a native woman named Kelly White, a friend and intimate of Craven, issued a press release under the IHRAAM heading. It claimed falsely that Kevin Annett was attempting to name himself as leader and mouthpiece for native people, and had no authority to do so.

Although the Tribunal came to an end amid this sort of conflict and sabotage, we had achieved a historic success, in publicly documenting crimes against humanity in the residential schools for the first time. We had video-recorded some fourteen hours of testimony, and I had assembled a stack of affidavits and documentation corroborating those statements, gathered from government archives and other sources at the University.

Two days after the Tribunal, I personally packaged both the videos and the documentation and shipped everything to Mary Robinson, as High Commissioner for Human Rights for the United Nations in Geneva.

IHRAAM had been delegated to issue its own report on the Tribunal, so having dispatched the transcript material to Geneva, I sought out Rudy James. Over coffee in a drab little café on East Hastings Street, he looked at me blankly. He seemed drawn and tired.

'So when are you and the judges going to submit your own reports?' I began as he stirred his coffee and looked out the fly-specked window.

'I've been suspended by IHRAAM,' he said. 'The jury's still out on Diana.'

I couldn't believe it.

'What the hell for?'

He shrugged. 'Jim Craven registered a formal complaint accusing me of "indecent behavior". You remember that rumor about me making out with one of the witnesses?'

'I know. I'd attributed that little gem to Ed John's boys.'

'Somebody,' said Rudy, 'has done a totally professional job of discrediting our Tribunal, Kevin. Did you notice the unmarked van outside the hall each day?'

The sabotage had been so effective that I had to believe it had been put together by someone with resources beyond those of a tribal council, or of casual objectors.

'We've still got the Geneva office to hear from.'

Rudy nodded.

'Before I got my bad news, I notified the Human Rights Office in Geneva that our Tribunal had found the government of Canada, the RCMP and the Catholic, United and Anglican churches guilty of crimes against humanity.

I recommended that Mary Robinson launch a formal inquiry into the residential schools, hopefully to lay charges at the International Criminal Court.'

'Here's hoping,' I said. His look said it all.

We never heard back from Mary Robinson's office. We were to learn that pressure from a UN diplomat named Louise Frechette – a former Canadian civil servant, and right-hand person close to UN Secretary-General Koffi Annan – had shut down the High Commissioner's Office, and IHRAAM itself.

Our Tribunal got a scant mention in only one newspaper, the *Globe and Mail's* issue on June 20, 1998.

Meanwhile, the fallout from the Tribunal began to hit many who had testified. People who had spoken were beaten up, evicted from their homes on the reservations, and denied financial assistance by band councils. Even death threats were said to have been made.

Two weeks after the Tribunal, an RCMP tactical squad broke into Harriet Nahanee's home on the Squamish reservation and held everyone at gunpoint for an hour while the house was ransacked. Absolutely trashed. There was no search warrant.

Shortly afterward, I discovered – fortunately when I was driving slowly on a city street – that the brake line of my own car had been severed. And I was subsequently followed by two men, on two separate occasions, who physically assaulted me.

Such melodrama was not accidental. The two key witnesses who described native-run pedophilia among the Carrier Nation chiefs were arrested without a warrant and held in Vancouver for more than a week. On their release, without any charges having been laid, they were evicted from their house on the reservation and beaten up by envoys from Ed John's Carrier band council.

The full viciousness of this aftermath descended on me. An internet campaign that continues to the present day succeeded in blacklisting me and destroying the Circle of Justice. All of this thwarted my efforts, for a time. But in the ruin of this latest sabotage, I could only ask myself, for there was no one else to ask,

'What the hell do I do now?'

29

March 2002 – Vancouver Island

Saanich is a pleasant suburb on Vancouver Island, just north of the provincial capital of Victoria. There, as part of a high school history program, six senior students led by a seventeen-year-old girl called Nicole Turcotte, in their reading about west coast history, learn about Reverend Kevin Annett. One of them hears him on a public radio broadcast from Vancouver. Nicole is delegated to invite him to speak to their history class and he accepts.

This is the first time Kevin Annett has been asked to lecture to high school students, and while, after years in the pulpit, he is no stranger to large audiences, he is surprised on his arrival to find that the small history class has attracted the attention of the entire high school's 200 students, who are assembled in the school's auditorium to hear his words.

As he proceeds with a review of the events of the previous ten years, particularly the history of the residential schools there on Vancouver Island, he is an instant success with the Saanich High School. To cheers and a standing ovation, Kevin calls on the students to support his efforts to bring Canada and its churches to trial for genocide.
In the aftermath of his prolonged lecture and question period, Nicole and her friends are so aroused in their youthful outrage that they decide to demonstrate at the upcoming United Church Annual Meeting in Victoria, a scant ten miles away.

Arriving at the Victoria conference hall, and not content with a protest demonstration outside the building, Nicole and the others move inside the church meeting, since it is held in a public space. They quietly walk in and, taking seats among the church youth delegates, they begin circulating material and informing the attendees of the residential school atrocities for which their church is responsible.

'We were only there a few minutes,' says Nicole in a later radio interview, *'when this big guy comes over and grabs me by the shoulder. He and a couple of other guys haul us up out of our chairs and drag us over to the door. My arm was really hurting, the way he was twisting it.*

'The big guy and his friends turn out to be church officials and he tells us we're not allowed on the premises. So I say to him: "Why not? This is a free country, and we have a right to be in a public place under the Charter of Rights and Freedoms."
'So guess what he says? "The Charter of Rights and Freedoms doesn't apply here. We're the United Church of Canada!"'
On past performance, Kevin tells Nicole, the big guy is right. In the case of the United Church of Canada, the Charter of Rights and Freedoms is null and void.

30
1999 – An Interregnum

In the year immediately following the abortive IHRAAM Tribunal, it seemed to me that an iron cage had descended on me. Everything I had achieved was scattered to the winds. The media imposed a blackout on the whole topic of residential schools. Many of my contacts stopped speaking to me. The death threats multiplied, and a fresh campaign against me and my work launched across the country caused most people to back right away – even those who knew the truth. People were afraid, and unwilling to say why.

All of this came about through a massive public relations campaign by the United Church of Canada and federal institutions, epitomized by a 'press advisory' issued by the United Church's head office early in 1999, in response to a tiny article about our Tribunal that appeared in the *New Internationalist* magazine in the U.K.

Composed by national church officer David Iverson, the fourteen-page 'advisory' referred not once to any of the evidence or allegations against his church concerning crimes in their residential schools. Indians were not even mentioned. The release, rather, was a detailed character assassination of me, complete with lengthy quotations from the United Church's 'delisting report' that purported to be the final assessment of me and my ministry. Without providing any evidence, Iverson described me as mentally unstable, prone to fabricating evidence, and universally despised and rejected by native people.

The Canadian media, not prone to investigate the truth, swallowed this elaborate nostrum and for years would not even print my letters or even interview eyewitnesses to sterilizations and other hitherto unreported crimes, all of which I had lined up.

Without exception, the media meekly continued their policy of the previous five years. With canine curiosity, they had initially sniffed around the edges of what they perceived as an opportunity to improve circulation, but with the more recent sound of a commanding corporate voice, they contented themselves with lifting a collective hind leg over the residential schools issue, and then trotting off in pursuit of their normal coverage of worldwide oddities and community trivia.

Those native people who had so courageously come forward with testimony at the Tribunal were almost without exception harassed, hounded, financially and physically punished, by persons often, but not always, unknown.

Even as far away as Boulder, Colorado, Royce and Lydia White Calf, who had served as two of the more forceful and sympathetic tribunal judges, and who alone had issued their own report of the Tribunal's findings, were subjected for years afterward to strange and unexplainable verbal and physical harassment.

The counter-attack didn't stop there. The very group that Harriet and I had founded and which made the Tribunal possible, the Circle of Justice, was destroyed from within by a professional campaign. Four members of our former Circle of Justice were asked by Jim Craven to denounce me publicly and to claim that I had used their statements without permission. They were even offered payment to do so, with the assertion that he had the backing of the Canadian government. The result was to drive away many native people who had worked with me.

And with the hammer, of course, always comes the glove. Alongside these attacks against the few of us who tried to surface the truth of the Tribunal's findings, there followed a concerted effort by the Canadian government and the churches to buy off and silence the survivors with a $350 million 'Aboriginal Healing Fund', created just months after our Tribunal.

With this fund, a new and novel page was turned, with a system of more widespread payoff and bribery, designed to appear as compensation for the sins of the past. This program would be expanded in subsequent years commensurate with the rising level of lawsuits against church and state.

I preferred to call the whole payoff the 'Aboriginal Hush Fund', especially when it was revealed that applicants could only access the Fund if they had not previously sued the government or the churches, and would consent to sign off from any such litigation and confine their activity to personal 'healing' issues. Read: Take the money and shut up, or else!

When it wasn't buying silence, the federal government continued to remain as aloof as ever. Its perennially popular francophone Prime Minister, Jean Chretien, the surname perhaps convincingly redolent of his devout Christianity, had been unsuccessfully 'subpoenaed' by the IHRAAM Tribunal, along with thirty-three other church and state officials who had ignored the diplomatic summons. Some time later, that PM would distinguish himself as the only head of state in the western world who failed to offer condolences to his American neighbors on the death of 3,000 people on the occasion known as 9/11; and as the man who ordered that protestors be forcibly assaulted and silenced by RCMP goons with pepper spray during the notorious APEC Summit in Vancouver.

The RCMP continued its well-rehearsed policy of refusing to investigate any claims about crimes at residential schools, save for issuing veiled threats to me that I should tread carefully with revelations about dead children.

The United Church, seemingly not content with the attempted destruction of my life and that of my family, and subsequently trashing my attempt to bring our news to the world, suddenly became the Indians' best friend, with a plethora of plans for 'healing and reconciliation'. Apparently, despite their successful trashing of the truth and the innocent, people in the upper church echelons remained apprehensive, like any criminal still at large.

For me, these developments served only to accentuate the futility of my situation. It seemed that I was destined to face total defeat during that final year of the twentieth century.

It was time for me to step back, assess the damage and determine what, if anything, was still possible.

When the emotional smoke began to clear for me, I realized that nothing really essential had been lost. I was still intact, healthy, and much wiser about the way of the world, especially concerning what I faced. Most importantly, I had kept my honor and integrity.

I still held in my hands the most potent weapon of all: the raw truth – and even more so now, in the wake of the Tribunal. This truth now included the hundreds of testimonies from residential school survivors, combined with the documentation I was daily uncovering from Indian Affairs archives at UBC.

I knew that I had the substance of an earth-shattering message in my hands. The world simply had to learn what had happened in those horror-ridden 'schools'. In fact it was not just an opportunity, but rather my obligation and purpose to find a means of delivering that message. I owed it to all of the children who had suffered, living and dead, to let their voices finally be heard. And I owed it to my own children, who were ten and seven by then, and beginning to come into awareness of what they and their father had suffered.

My eldest daughter Clare summed up this growing recognition one Sunday as she and Elinor and I drove home from a joyous day at Kitsilano Beach. Staring out the window at the homeless people scattered all over East Hastings Street, Clare turned to me and with an angry look said,

'Daddy, I thought we fed all those people! Why are they still hungry?'

Remembering our happy sojourns together to deliver bread at

the Alberni Indian reserves when she was barely four years old, I looked at her soberly and said, 'They're kept that way deliberately, Clare. They're Indians, mostly, and our people have been trying to kill them off for a long time.'

My words clearly troubled her, but more and more she began asking me about my work, and the people on those mean streets.

With everything that had happened, I set out in the summer of 1999 to compile a definitive dossier which would ultimately include a comprehensive website, a radio program, and an award-winning documentary film, consisting of nothing less than the first independent and thorough documentation of genocide in Canada. It would eventually serve as a basis of a national movement that would earn international attention.

Fortune smiled on me then, as it has always done at the most crucial moments. In the summer of 1999, I met a woman named Pamela Holm, who offered me a quiet and idyllic place to live and work on Salt Spring Island in the Gulf of Georgia. There I settled in to organize and compile a body of work that would be my first book, entitled *Hidden from History: The Canadian Holocaust.*

The book would take nearly a year to complete, but ultimately it would begin to turn the tables on the Goliath that had destroyed so many of our lives.

31
The New Millennium – Salt Spring Island, Canada

All you have to do, his inner voice tells him, is to make it increasingly uncomfortable for the bad guys. Everything else will follow.

That's all very well and good, he replies, but all the familiar barriers are still present: my marginalization from help, the public and media apathy and the continual pressure of my own grinding poverty... not to mention the implacable presence, always sensed if not felt, of well-funded adversaries.

He has learned to be stoic and realistic, somehow retaining trust, not dwelling on concern for himself or his poverty. Every month, slight bits of income or random donations appear, enabling him to carry on another step, or two. He uses these scraps of income to keep seeing his daughters, and maintaining a semblance of life with them, hiding his pain from them, or at least trying to. He is unable to find any full-time work: his total blacklisting has reached everywhere, invariably helped along by anonymous phone calls or dead-end referrals, so that prospective employers are quickly canceled out.

His only regret and his deepest pain is for his children, who are becoming young women now, and who have never known their father except as a struggling man; but one, of course, who has always been there for them, at every dance recital and school concert. He tries to avoid the caustic 'what if' scenarios that rob sleep and cause contempt to come up with the sun. But he is human, and very alone.

Several of his attempts at relationships with women have foundered on the rocks of his ordeal, and of his own refusal to expose his children to more pain. Few women can share his kind of life, of danger and sacrifice, except from a respectful, perhaps admiring, distance.

His work is increasingly well known in 'Indian country' and he responds to a slowly growing number of invitations to speak at healing circles and aboriginal conferences all over Canada. For the lid is gradually coming off the truth, as more survivors are encouraged by his work and public presence to share their darkest stories aloud.

Most of these invitations are inaccessible, because he is usually without the funds to travel. For a long time, he focuses his efforts where his effectiveness is possible: in the downtown east side of Vancouver, where so many survivors live, and among the native bands on Vancouver Island, where for him it all began, almost a full decade before.

Ensconced in the home of Pamela Holm, his new friend and cautious supporter, the calm of Salt Spring Island allows him to compose his first book and throw down a new gauntlet to his adversaries. The Beast, momentarily assuaged, stirs at this new threat.

32
2000–2001 – The West Coast

Life was beginning to move again for me as the new century dawned, back to a semblance of what was essential and restorative, after a whirlwind of pain and insanity. But I was changed now, stripped of the self-delusion I had called naivety, the impulse to trust that Goliath will listen to reason and not require a shot right between the eyes.

But now I was convinced that my Adversary's time had come, and that I was elected to be one of its executioners. Or perhaps an exorcist of a sort.

I had once taken part in an exorcism in Port Alberni, and what became clear to me, even at that time, was how unlike the possessed person the exorcist must be, in order that one spirit may expel another. Increasingly, I have assumed such a stance fighting against a power I consider to be analogous to a demonically possessed person: the culture in which I was raised and tutored, and which – in whatever guise – I must now help bring down.

By fighting it for so long, up close and outraged, I had become even more a part of it, entangled in its spirit and reflecting that so often unconsciously. Only when it expelled me and flung me far away from itself did I begin to recover, through pain and a refining process that laid bare the deep lie in which I had partaken.

Perhaps this was, again, like Nelson Mandela's long incarceration – the discovery that in total deprivation lies the beginning of our real growth and understanding.

During the first year of the new century, I began compiling the complete record of all that I had documented and uncovered up to then. My first aim was to reveal everything that I had learned, and was continuing to learn, about the Christian death camps known as 'Indian residential schools'. But I soon realized that what I was really constructing was a huge mirror in which my own people could see the evil they had really condoned, and within which they were continuing to live. I suddenly saw what I had been a part of: a monstrous slaughterhouse in which we survive only by seeing and feeling nothing around us. Eyeless in Gaza. But for some reason, one day my sight had been restored, and suddenly there had been illuminated for me a panorama of terror, by being exposed to its survivors.

The more I have wandered in this new land, the clearer its terrain has become, and the more I have met stumbling victims and those who continue to suffer its horrors. And yet ironically, the further I have gone, the darker has become the place I once inhabited: the comfortable, closeted world of a privileged culture and its triumphant powerful Christian Empire, and cheek by jowl with them those other souls who struggle within its darkness.

I tried for too long to communicate what I was discovering to those who languished in my old world, but it had proven to be impossible. My mainstream fellows not only find themselves incapable of imagining the horrors I have encountered; they simply don't want to know about them, regardless of their 'progressiveness'.

Within their numbed and addicted state, they see no reason why their own world should be shattered, any more than I would have before my transformation.. Any word as unsettling as 'genocide' to 'normal people' is not simply an abstraction, but an affront. Genocide happens in Kosovo, not Canada, after all. Any remote occurrence, such as the secret murder and burial of an Indian child, can at best be the concern of lawyers and government, not of churches and their adherents, and the whole mess must be pushed out of sight and out of mind.

When I sat down on Salt Spring Island and began to piece

together a lexicon containing the genocidal history of my own culture, I didn't realize initially that what I was doing was driving another stake into the heart of our delusion by saying, 'Look, we're not who we thought we were. We're part of a murderous lie. It's time to let the lie fade and die; it's time for us to become who we once were, who we really are.'

Before revealing the lie, I first had to document the truth. It took me nearly a year to pull together all of the testimonies, the documents and other proven sources dealing with the crimes Christian Canada had committed in Indian residential schools and hospitals.

The fact that my public work had been so completely sabotaged ultimately worked to my advantage in this task, for there were no longer any distractions, no rallies to organize, no people to counsel and support, which would have pulled me away, as it always had, from the careful job of documenting what had been entrusted and made available to me.

I became a deliberate recluse during the year 2000, researching, editing, compiling and typing, until finally, *Hidden from History: The Canadian Holocaust* existed as a solid body of evidence. I observed to myself, with a brief and ironic smile, that what I had achieved was originally intended to be my long-lost PhD dissertation, which the establishment had scuttled. But instead of gathering dust on a library shelf at UBC, it was now out in the world, as a weapon for the dispossessed.

I assembled the book around the United Nations' five definitions of genocide, systematically proving that all of the definitions – such as preventing childbirth, murder, kidnapping children and so on – had been deliberate, rampant and continuous in the Canadian residential schools for more than a century.

As I had anticipated, not a single member of the media or the publishing industry in Canada would dare touch my material. I offered it to dozens, all of whom responded with the same fear, the same comment: they had no appetite for being sued by government or church.

While discouraging to me at first, that response also worked to the ultimate advantage of the printed material, since I was forced to copy and distribute the book myself, and in so doing I removed any copyright restriction from it. I also did that intentionally, believing, as I still do, that what I have uncovered is public knowledge, not the property of anyone. This encouraged people, especially residential school survivors, to photocopy documents and other parts of my material in order to help them in their recovery, and also in their court cases.

Everything I had put together was immediately accessible to native people across Canada, hundreds of whom began photocopying and circulating parts of it throughout their communities. Ultimately, part or all of it was shared in this way, all over the world.

This material was explosive in its effect, because many residential school survivors were just beginning to struggle in court to present their claims against the government and the churches.

As one small example, a document that I reproduced called the 'Application for Admission' form, which all native parents had been forced to sign on pain of jail time, revealed that the residential school principal was the legal guardian of all native students, and therefore was liable, along with his church, for all the harm that was done to native children under his care. That document was an immediate success in the courtrooms, and helped establish that the churches were equally liable, along with the government, for all that had befallen the schools' inmates.

Soon after the completion of my work early in 2001, I saw firsthand how this one document was helping survivors deal with their old wounds far better than all their sessions with counselors and other professional fixers. It happened one spring day in the long house of the Nanaimo Indian band, where a healing circle of survivors from the Kuper Island Catholic residential school were gathered with their families around a large fire.

The dozen survivors were all aging, one woman being eighty-four years old, but they all still carried the deep scars of their childhood torture at Kuper Island: a particularly notorious facility where children had been routinely flogged, sterilized, killed and used in grisly medical experiments.

The fact that one of the men in the circle described seeing his little sister thrown to her death from a window by a nun was starkly horrifying enough. But to draw the inevitable conclusion, the realization that such an event was not an isolated tragedy, but a single stitch in a fabric of planned slaughter, was overwhelming.

And it was into this circle of suffering that I stepped that day with a copy of the Application for Admission Form, which I had earlier discovered in the Koerner Library at UBC.

I told the survivors that they should not blame themselves or their parents anymore, as some of them had described having done, because of the nightmare they had endured. Holding up the form, I said,

'This was the law that stole you from your parents. They couldn't come and rescue you because they weren't your legal guardians any longer. It wasn't their fault.'

The eighty-four-year-old woman immediately broke into sobs, as did some of the others. After some time, she came to me, took the form, and tossed it into the flames. She sighed, faintly smiled, and sat down. It was as if a shroud had been lifted from the gathering as the smoke from the consumed paper floated skywards.

'Healing' is a cheap word, easily dispensed, but rarely manifested. I have had the honor of witnessing it sprout, in the most unlikely places, but only once it's been watered by risk, and suffering, and sacrifice.

33
April 27, 2002 – Vancouver, Canada

On this day, CTV, the second largest national television network in Canada, airs for the first time a program consisting of stories told by first-hand witnesses to murder in west coast residential schools. The program is entitled First Story, and includes interviews with Reverend Kevin Annett and more than a dozen aboriginal survivors of Roman Catholic, Anglican and United Church schools.

It is the first occasion in which the media mentions some of the atrocities the survivors endured. And on the same program, Dr Brian Thorpe, the former chief executive officer of the United Church of Canada's BC Conference, who helped destroy Kevin Annett's career and family and is now a national church officer, is quoted as saying:

'We know that criminal acts occurred in the residential schools ... anything is possible.' The Reverend Kevin Annett, participating in the program, observes to his interviewer that the very words Dr Thorpe is now pronouncing as an official spokesman for the United Church are precisely the same words which, five years earlier, resulted in that church's defrocking and public ex-communication of him, and contributed to his total loss of livelihood, and that of his family.

Currently, the United Church is adopting a new strategy of 'healing' and 'outreach', offering 'healing funds' to church-allied native groups, and providing other evidence of its self-proclaimed tradition of 'reconciliation'.

In the full spirit of this sudden concern, the United Church Observer, the church's official national publication, will shortly feature in full color on its front page the pudgy-cheeked, smiling countenance of a happy Indian child.

34
Interlude – On Conquest, Reconciliation and Re-Subordination

Faith does not require great intelligence.
Catholic Archbishop Raymond Roussin,
Vancouver Archdiocese, January 19, 2007

I used to love Sunday school when I was a kid in Winnipeg, mostly because of Constance Peterson, a fellow eight-year-old who I was secretly in love with. But Connie and her glorious smile upped and moved to Brandon during my tenure with her at Wentworth United Church, which ended my pre-pubescent longings and made me ask myself what I was doing there.

Perhaps it was my unexpected childhood grief that started me listening to what Mrs Lowe, the erstwhile teacher, was trying to cram into our bored little heads about the Bible. What I heard didn't make a hell of a lot of sense to me.

Take Genesis, chapter one. How it all began.

What I heard from Mrs Lowe's stern lips was that some strange deity, or deities (both terms are used) decided to create people, but with pretty fearful and confused motives, since these deities gave us brains but ordered us never to use them. That Tree of Knowledge is strictly off bounds: we want you innocent and stupid, folks. Naturally, being human, we used our smarts anyway, got aware, and were punished for it: we got booted from our home like wayward kids, into a life of permanent misery. Not only that, but all of creation got damned in the process.

'And why?' poor Mrs Lowe muttered at the cluster of us scared, confused tikes.

'Because of human sin and disobedience!'

Okay, so it's all our fault.

What crap, I thought. How does an all-powerful deity get off blaming his own handiwork for his mistake? That sounds a lot like my mother.

Years later, when for some masochistic reason I found myself a seminarian and struggling to understand Hebrew, I looked up the original meaning of the Genesis creation story, and found that I had been lied to in a serious way. In fact, what I discovered was that a wholly different story lies hidden within the original Hebrew language version of Genesis which is quite at odds with the standard, English biblical account.

I blamed Mrs Lowe at first, and my mother. But then I realized that a huge industry has been at work for millennia to hide from us some basic truth about who we are.

The usual version of creation has 'god' creating something out of nothing, right in the very first sentence of the Bible: 'In the beginning, God created the heaven and the earth'. But that's not what the Hebrew says. The word 'created' is *bara* in Hebrew, which means 'to cut down'. God 'cut down' the heavens and the earth?

It gets better. Where the English version says, 'Now the earth was empty and without form', the Hebrew expression for 'without form' is *tohuw*, which means 'to lay waste'. That's an active verb. In short, god didn't create the earth: he found one already around, and laid waste to it and destroyed it.

This god sounds like a psychopathic warlord!

Sometime in my second year at the Vancouver School of Theology, training for the ministry, I sat down with my inter-linear Bible and lexicon, and I translated the entire Genesis account. Here's the story I came up with:

At one period in history, some powerful entities called the Eloyhim waged war against the earth and utterly destroyed it, creating desolation and nothingness. They imposed darkness, sorrow, evil and death on creation. That which was once whole and harmonious was torn completely in two by the Eloyhim, who established a bipolar universe of opposites.

Into this turbulence the Eloyhim then created a species of artificial people that resembled them but lacked their wisdom and substance. These phantom-like robots mirrored the falseness of the chaos created by the Eloyhim, and were placed on the earth with strict orders not to seek knowledge or become aware of what was happening around them, or of who they really were. Yet, helped along by other creatures, the artificial people sought and achieved consciousness anyway, became fully aware beings, and discovered that they were exactly the same as the all-powerful ones who had invented them, the Eloyhim.

In response, the Eloyhim, terrified that they would be overthrown by their creations, crafted an enormous lie to so confuse and traumatize the newly aware human race that it would never be able to know its true identity and nature again, as fully god-like entities. The Eloyhim banished humanity into the world and burdened them with sorrow, shame, self-hatred and fear, blaming them for their fate, their 'fall', and for the 'cursing' of all creation.

What the Bible describes as humanity's original sin was simply our gaining of full consciousness, what it calls 'the knowledge of good and evil'. How could acquiring such knowledge be an evil act, except to those threatened by it, like the Eloyhim?

To make their vengeance on an awakened race complete, the Eloyhim brainwashed our ancestors through fear to live in the world as conquerors and destroyers, repeating the violence of the Eloyhim themselves: we were taught that creation is our enemy, and ordered to 'multiply and fill the earth and subdue it, and all its creatures': *kabash*, the Hebrew word for 'subdue', means literally to tread down, conquer, violate, disregard and bring into bondage.

Hello, genocide. Hello, ecocide.

The shame of humanity is not that of being aware and knowledgeable, as the Bible and the church teaches, but is the false consciousness sown in us by our oppressors. All throughout the true Genesis message that lies hidden within the church's account is the fact that god, not the serpent, is the enemy of humanity, that what the Eloyhim/'God' called evil was in fact a good thing, and that our rising to our full humanity was condemned and punished by a sick and corrupted deity.

It took a few days for my discovery to sink in, but one day on the beach I remember feeling that the sky had opened up wide and my mind had suddenly leapt to some new, incredible level. Holy shit! I thought. I am part of an enormous lie! What the church calls the word of God is actually the opposite: the word of a Deceiver.

Genesis, you see, is the basic paradigm of European-Christian, and hence global, culture. And the essential message of Genesis is that we are evil and corrupt people who deserve all the shit we get; that we can never be perfect or get better by ourselves, but only through the intervention of God, and specifically the self-appointed rulers who claim to speak for God; and that the world and everyone and all creatures in it are not good and complete in themselves, but need constant and forcible improvement and correction.

Talk about a recipe for permanent war, conquest and desecration. And that, according to the original meaning of Genesis, is precisely what the oppressive Eloyhim, whom we call 'God', want for us.

Jesus, we are told, is the way out of this whole mess – at least for a 'Christian'. He somehow 'reconciles' us to the power-hungry sicko who put us here, the God-Eloyhim. But is that a good thing?

Maybe to the Eloyhim, and their churchly apologists. After all, every tyrant wants to see his rebellious people come crawling back and asking for forgiveness, and to be restored to slavery. For that is the original wrong of humanity, according to the church: that we 'rebelled' against God by trying to think for ourselves and know our true identity. That's why the term 'reconciliation' is so interesting, and of enormous significance.

The term 'reconciliation' is not what it seems, which in the common usage is when two opponents bury the hatchet and come to terms with one another. The actual meaning is the very opposite of this, referring to when a rebellious party is subdued and makes penance to his former ruler.

Backtrack in time to the high Middle Ages, when the Roman Catholic Church launched its first major crusade against 'Saracens and pagans', that is, anyone who wasn't a Catholic Christian. A legal system was needed to justify the church's conquest and slaughter of all those Others – including, one day, indigenous peoples all over the planet. So Vatican lawyers cooked up something called an 'indulgence', a brilliant device that made it a virtue to loot, rape and murder when these acts were done in the name of the church.

In 1095, Pope Urban II declared that Christian Crusaders in the Middle East were absolved from any consequences for crimes committed in the upcoming war against Muslims, and in fact were restored to a state of original innocence and sinlessness, by waging such a war! Religious violence suddenly became a virtue, under church law.

It's that wiping away of 'original sin' through violence that has me so intrigued. For by this law, the church arrogated to itself the original powers of the Eloyhim themselves: the power to declare that human beings were not in fact sinful. Why? Because our 'sin' gets rubbed out when we do what the Eloyhim intended for us: to conquer and kill in the name of the Eloyhim, as represented by the church.

Cast in the role of the Eloyhim, all the suddenly reprieved Christians get to slaughter without shame or blame, as is still the case today when it comes to crimes committed by the church and its agents. And, accordingly, all those 'unbelievers' damaged by the Crusaders had no basis to claim that any wrong was done to them, since the opponents of the Eloyhim-church were, like the original Adam and Eve, the cause of their own downfall. And as such, these enemies of the church have had to make special restitution to the latter for having caused the violence done against them!

This act of restitution by the conquered was termed a *reconciliation*.

During the Spanish Inquisition, for example, Catholics who had 'lapsed' and become Lutherans were 'reconciled through loss of property and compelled to endure prison terms'. In 1612, five citizens of Madrid were 'subjected' to reconciliation for practicing Judaism and committed to the galleys as slaves. To quote the medieval historian Henry Charles Lea,

'Reconciliation to the Church entailed confiscation and was usually accompanied with other penalties according to the record of the culprit and the readiness with which he confessed and recanted. There might be prison, public humiliation, scourging or the galleys.'

In effect, the rebel *indemnifies* the conqueror (sound familiar?) by acknowledging that the violence and injustices done by the latter were right and necessary, thus freeing the conqueror from blame, shame or liability: that is, stating publicly that no crime had been committed, except by the conquered and re-subjected rebel.

This notion and practice of blaming a victim for their suffering at the hands of a ruler, and of expecting any rebel or opponent to do penance on the ruler's terms, is the core message of the church's version of Genesis. It's a theme that is also basic to Roman and Greek philosophical belief that the mighty are always right, that power equals virtue, and that the conquered have no rights or status and must make amends to the conqueror.

The Romans institutionalized this belief through their religious rites wherein conquered chieftains or other enemies of Rome sought forgiveness on their knees in front of the Emperor, prior to their public strangulation. And as the direct heir of the Roman Empire, the Roman Catholic Church incorporated this practice into its treatment of any enemy it conquered, including dissident Christians, Jews, Muslims or indigenous people.

The essence of this practice – the public indemnification of the ruler by his victims and the condemnation and killing of the latter – is simply the acting out of the church's most basic paradigm: the supposed 'fall' of humanity and the need for our 'reconciliation' with the Eloyhim ('God') as re-subjected slaves. But as we now know, this entire paradigm is a fraudulent misinterpretation and distortion of the actual Genesis message.

All of this struck home to me in the spring of 2009, as I watched the pathetic groveling of government Indian 'Chief' Phil Fontaine in front of the Pope in Rome, after the latter had issued a holocaust-denying 'regret' for 'some' of the harms caused in Indian boarding schools. Not only did poor Phil kiss the papal ring (and undoubtedly other parts) but he joyfully 'accepted' the Pope's statement as 'proof that healing has finally arrived'.

Like any conquered chief seeking resubmission to the fold before his public execution (Phil was removed as AFN Chief a month or so after his papal audience), Phil Fontaine was simply re-enacting, like the Pope, an ancient ritual of surrender that the conquerors like to call 'reconciliation'.

35
2002–2003 – Vancouver, Canada

Within the year following completion of Hidden from History, *small successes follow in rapid succession, like buds returning after a long cold snap. Kevin Annett prints the book by himself and circulates it to libraries, human rights groups and native people everywhere. Nelson Mandela receives a copy, and the book is quoted at the United Nations by Belgian emissaries, who chide Canada for its own genocide. But for the most part it finds its way to small and unnoticed places, among the people who need the truth the most.*

Kevin Annett is invited to establish a weekly talk radio program entitled 'Hidden from History' at Vancouver Co-op Radio, situated in the heart of skid row where his supporters mostly reside. At the same time, he helps found the Truth Commission into Genocide in Canada, designed to pick up where the IHRAAM Tribunal was halted.
The Truth Commission is the first and only public organization in Canada to confront the issue of atrocities in the residential schools honestly, long before it becomes politically fashionable to mention the subject. It is the actual predecessor to all of the later efforts to bring 'healing' and 'justice' to survivors.

At the same time, Kevin founds a street church in neighboring New Westminster among native and low-income people. It is known as All Peoples' Church.

The common thread that runs through each of these developments is the mushrooming connections he continues to make with residential school survivors. The continuing campaign against him cannot penetrate to the street, for the hush money and government muscle does not extend there. An increasing number of those survivors begin attending his church services and listening to his radio program, continually aiding in the process of documenting stories of terror and murder in the residential schools and their adjoining hospitals.

Buoyed by this enthusiasm, Kevin begins to organize protest rallies and prayer vigils outside Roman Catholic, Anglican and United Churches in downtown Vancouver. Most of the participants are these street-level survivors and other native people. Few whites, however 'progressive', will associate themselves with Kevin Annett and his work.

Predictably, all of these means of elevating public awareness prompt an immediate initiative by both church and state once again, in an attempt to bury the issue of the residential schools. Once again, the avenue employed is the cadre the government maintains among senior native politicians.

'In Latin America,' his doomed friend Fidel said one night in Chiapas many years earlier, 'they deal with dissident leaders by shooting them. In your country, they put them on the payroll.' Brother Fidel's words are prophetic, in the years immediately following the new attention Kevin and his people are beginning to attract. The increasing protests catalyzed by the release of so much documented evidence is now countered by a deluge of government spending and 'healing funds', largely to chiefs and tribal councils who could potentially take the next step and start naming the names.

'Healing fund' is an oddly ambiguous yet predictable expression, coming from a culture of strip malls and convenience. It implies that the worst imaginable atrocities and human agony may be assuaged by monetary payments. It implies that money is a resolution, that 'healing' takes place within the victim as a result. It may logically be asserted that the healing, if any, occurs solely within the conscience and the legal liability of the donor.

Credit for devising the expression – and the program – should right-fully be accorded the white lawyers who invariably were present as intermediaries, that is to say, greasers of the wheels of 'justice'. Inevitably, as in most legal practices, most of the lubricant adheres to the hands of the lubricators.

In distributing this compensation, the perpetrators of the crimes strive to dictate to their victims the terms of the latter's 'healing', defining for them what is just, and how they are to recover. It is a simple replication of the historical method of colonizing: of dictating the terms, of finally 'fixing the heathens' with yet another device to control and subjugate them.

One survivor, a homeless man on Vancouver's skid row, sums it up shortly after the government's largesse is announced: 'After I pay the fuckin' lawyer, there's just enough left over to get drunk on or o.d. before I commit suicide.'

For most Canadians, and certainly for the churchgoers, the most sure defense mechanism is a simple dissociation, mentally removing themselves from any connection with the residential schools, what created them, and what happened there, just as effectively as if that evil had been planned and perpetrated by some remote third party. A 'healing fund' is a way to make the dissociation complete.

Meanwhile, the churches and government officials across Canada spend months and years intent on 'healing' their victims while refusing to acknowledge the deaths and torture caused by them in the first place: an enigma as deranged as that of a serial killer who convinces himself that he didn't actually harm anyone, although he is willing to make restitution to his victims' relatives.

With no upheaval and turmoil, with no healthy cognitive dissonance which might be required for any real recognition and change to occur, any shred of remorse is totally missing in an individual, a church or state. Psychologists say that without such discomfort and self-evaluation, a numb insensitivity takes over and the subject must withdraw from the reality of how he is affecting and hurting others, in the manner of an untreated psychopath. Any real healing is therefore impossible.

Often, as Kevin Annett stands outside a church on a Sunday morning with a few others, handing leaflets to the scattered parishioners trudging into huge and empty cathedrals, it is common for him to be confronted with cries such as:

'We've dealt with this issue! We paid them lots of money! What more do they want?'

'It never benefits the people who need it,' someone will reply, 'and money doesn't help children who died in the residential schools…'

'Oh, that's garbage!' a proper church lady will scream back, decorum gone. 'My church didn't kill anybody!'

A few years later, when the government through the media acknowledges more of the crimes, including deaths, it will become more difficult for churches and adherents to claim that nobody died. But the denial continues, shifting and evasive, so that the mainstream's self-image is protected.

36
February 2003 – Censorship at the University of BC

During the month I turned forty-seven, I was invited to speak on the campus where I had seen my doctoral degree scuttled after church intervention. Richard Fredericks, an assistant professor of sociology at UBC, asked me to speak to his undergraduate criminology class on the research I'd done into crimes against humanity in Canada.

'No one else has dared to research what you have, Kevin, and I don't want to deal just with Bosnia and Rwanda when it comes to genocide,' Richard had told me over the phone.

Well and good. Despite my trepidation at experiencing a repeat shutdown, I agreed to give five lectures, and in late February, I spoke to his class of forty students. My talk was very well received, and they all looked forward to my next presentation.

Unfortunately, it never happened.

Two days after my initial lecture, I received a nervous phone call from Professor Fredericks, who told me that he was withdrawing his offer for me to speak to any more of his classes. Fredericks seemed to be in a very agitated and depressed state. He said: 'One of my students has made a complaint about your lecture,' but said nothing more.

'Why,' I asked him, 'would a single complaint from an undergraduate student require the canceling of my lectures?'

Professor Fredericks responded: 'I can't go into it right now.' I never did receive the promised honorarium payment for my sole lecture, and I forgot about the incident, until late in May of that year, when I received an e-mail message from Professor Fredericks asking that I meet with him.

He saw me in a coffee shop in downtown Vancouver. He

looked even worse than he had sounded on the phone, and he kept glancing around nervously as we spoke. He began by saying, 'The shit has really hit the fan.' Then, for more than an hour, he told me what had happened.

My lectures to Richard Fredericks' sociology class had been canceled as a direct result of the intervention of officials of the United Church of Canada with the senior members of the administration at the University of British Columbia. The United Church officials in question had threatened legal action against UBC unless they were assured that I would be prevented from lecturing at the University.

In addition, in the wake of my lecture, Professor Fredericks was reprimanded by officials of his own department for inviting me to speak to his class in the first instance, and he was forced to remove any material or reference to genocide in Canada from his 'Crimes against Humanity' course. He was also placed on effective probation within his department following my lecture, and an interim session course was removed from his normal teaching load.

In effect, not only was I effectively banned from lecturing at UBC, but Professor Fredericks had been officially censured and penalized for having invited me to speak. He was thereafter academically censored in terms of what he could and could not teach in his course on genocide.

In the course of Frederick's hour-long talk with me in May of 2003, and at subsequent occasions on which we met, he disclosed certain other information related to these events:

The initial complaint against me and my first lecture had been made not by one of Professor Frederick's students, but by the mother of one of the students, Louise Mangan, who was a United Church minister in Vancouver and a former classmate of mine at seminary. Upon hearing from her son about my lecture on the evening of its presentation, Mangan had contacted the BC Conference office of the United Church of Canada and spoken to its legal counsel, Jon Jessiman – who had played an instrumental role in my firing and expulsion from the United Church seven years earlier.

Also taking part in these discussions was an unnamed church official who was the next-door neighbor of a senior UBC administrator, and the former head of the Sociology Department, by the name of Neil Guppy.

On the basis of both informal discussion with these church officials, and a formal complaint brought by the United Church and addressed to UBC President Martha Piper, Neil Guppy, in his official capacity as Vice-President for Academic Affairs, directed the head of the UBC Anthropology-Sociology Department, Dr David Pokotylo (who had been one of my professors during my undergraduate years, and who knew me well), to meet with Richard Fredericks and instruct him not only to cancel my series of lectures in his class, but also to change the content of his curriculum on genocide in Canada.

This meeting between Dr Pokotylo and Professor Fredericks occurred approximately one week following my initial lecture, and as a result, my lectures were canceled and Richard Fredericks was placed under a form of discipline and censorship by his department.

'At my meeting with Dr Pokotylo,' Fredericks told me, 'he gave me the clear impression that unless I removed any reference to Canada from my curriculum material on genocide, I would not receive tenure or promotion within the department. He said that he "wasn't ordering" me, but that he was giving me the opportunity to refrain gracefully from teaching anything about the "so-called" Canadian genocide. I realized that I had to go along with him if I was to keep my job.' At the same meeting, Dr Pokotylo indicated to Fredericks that he was personally not in support of what was being asked of Fredericks, but that the matter was 'out of his hands', and the order to ban me and to discipline Fredericks was coming from both Neil Guppy, as Vice-

President of Academic Affairs, and the President's Office at the University of British Columbia.

As a result of his discussion with Pokotylo, Richard Fredericks complied with the pressure being brought against him, and not only canceled further lectures by me, but voluntarily modified the curriculum content of his course to exclude any reference to genocide in Canada.

But despite his compliance, Fredericks found himself increasingly marginalized and ostracized within the department, and subsequently was denied teaching appointments and other assignments. Richard Fredericks eventually decided to withdraw from teaching at the University of BC, and found new employment as a sessional instructor at Malaspina College in Nanaimo during the following year.

During the same period following my banning from further lecturing at UBC, that is, after the spring of 2003, I encountered a growing 'rumor-mongering' campaign against me among academics and organizations on the UBC campus, people who had formerly supported my work and public lectures. It seemed to me that an intensified campaign of vilification of me and my research was being organized on the UBC campus during the period following the censuring of Professor Fredericks.

On the basis of these events, I wrote a letter of complaint to the offices of both Neil Guppy and Martha Piper, respectively, the Vice-President for Academic Affairs and the President of UBC. My letter was a formal protest against the serious attack on free inquiry and academic freedom at UBC, and on the basic human rights of both myself and Professor Richard Fredericks. I accused them of allowing that attack to emanate from their respective offices.

I received no reply to my letter from either of them, nor to a second letter, this time registered, which I sent several weeks later.

The whole incident is still generally unknown among UBC

faculty and students, including among the plethora of 'activist' groups on campus. Genocide at home, clearly, is not an item on any scholarly agenda in Canada.

37
November 16, 2003 – East Side, Vancouver, Canada

The only antidote I have ever found to censorship has been in vocal, sustained protest, and on the very home turf of the perpetrators and those powers in control.

On this date, thirty of us, all of them aboriginal save me, calmly but resolutely took over the sanctuary of St James Anglican Church during its regular Sunday mass. Standing among and in front of the curious and shocked parishioners, and alongside outraged clergy, our small band unfurled a banner that declared,

'All the Children Need a Proper Burial.'

The truth had come home, and been named where it mattered: this was all about the missing residential school children – and those who are responsible for their death.

One of our number, an older native man who had seen his brother murdered by an Anglican priest at the church's Alert Bay school, announced to the shocked worshipers that we were refusing to leave the building until the church told us when they would return the missing children for a proper burial.

I had learned by then that the white world would simply not listen to native people, but, even if they suspected that he was insane, they would on occasion listen to a fellow white man. And so when the police and reporters arrived at the church we had occupied that morning, the first person they spoke to was me, the one white guy there.

'You have to wrap this up,' a hulking police sergeant told me. 'It's against the law to disrupt a church service.'

'We aren't disrupting,' I answered. 'We're here to ask them why they got away with killing children.'

The cop was trying to digest that one when the native protesters all began to drum and chant, and at that point, some of the parishioners actually got up and joined in, shaking the hands of the protesters and standing with them. That really upset the priests, one of whom literally ran over to the big cop and demanded that he evict the Indians 'at once'.

The guy needn't have worried. A few moments later, on some unspoken cue, our group began to slowly walk out of the sanctuary as they continued to drum. Triumphantly, they left most of the churchgoers, and definitely the priests, shocked and insecure, for the first time, on their own turf.

'We lost fifty members because of what you people did that day!' implored one of the priests to me, some time later.

'Well, that's a start,' I said quietly back to him.

It was this kind of escalating protest in and outside Canadian churches that began ratcheting up the heat again on those responsible, right when they thought we had all gone away. And in response to our action that day, the national Anglican Church issued a stream of public denials and denunciations that would have made Richard Nixon proud. No child, according to the church PR people, ever died in an Anglican residential school. Presumably, only the Catholics and the United Church killed Indian kids.

Denial, and the will to disbelieve, is a human trait especially strong at a time of trauma.

As a minister, I often encounter it at deathbeds, as families refuse to accept that a life they have loved is over; or with adulterous husbands, trying to convince themselves that they have not violated anything, ultimately, and can always go home again. But in the case of the residential schools we are faced with an entire society that has contained and hidden the truth at every level.

As a result, mainstream Canadian society never has had to face the truth about what they have been a part of, just as the winners of a war have no need to answer for anything. Never, until we spoke of the murdered children not as 'native children', but as 'children'.

As much as I was helping finally to crack open the Great Canadian Secret, by this time the wear and tear of years of this struggle had left me desolated, and almost incapable of carrying on. Instinctively, in the spring of 2002, I had moved to the rural expanses of Maple Ridge, east of Vancouver. Distanced from the urban madness, in a house by a quiet river, peace began to return to me again, especially with the knowledge of having made the truth widely known. Inner stillness came first, followed by a new and quiet resolve over what remained a seemingly hopeless cause.

It was in this new home that I wrote my second book, a biographical account of my story, entitled *Love and Death in the Valley*, which was eventually published in the United States. Composing it forced me to reflect on everything that had happened to me, and see more clearly what I was to do in the future.

My daughters were reaching their teenage years, and as young women, they assumed a new relationship with me: certainly more curious about my life, and about what had befallen all of us when they were so young. Yet how hard it was, still, for me to tell Clare and Elinor the depth of what I had suffered, and what I still struggled with every day. How well I began to understand the tendency of survivors never to share the horror of the residential schools with their own children, lest the pain and sickness be passed on.

For this reason, few people ever recover from their torture: a fact that most of them readily admit, despite the industry of 'healing and reconciliation' that exhorts them to pretend that recovery is actually possible.

During this period, on every Indian reservation, the few families that rule the roost were showered with huge payments from the government publicized as 'healing money'. The funds never got to the actual survivors who were suffering and dying every day from the residual and intergenerational effects of the residential schools. Instead, a few corpulent chiefs would fly off to Hawaii with their families to attend 'healer training workshops'. In return, they would make their people sign off from any legal action against the federal governments and the churches.

Most of the people who had been working with me on our campaign had given up, by this point. I often joke about the 'thirty-day rule' when it comes to white people's interest in our work: that's usually how long their interest lasts in the whole topic of genocide in their own backyard. But even among native people, exposing the fact of dead children and planned ethnic cleansing was usually frowned upon, now that the 'official' native chiefs had derived all the benefit they could expect from the issue.

Despite all of this, and strengthened within by my new-found peace and resolve, I simply continued what I'd been doing for years: finding the evidence, making it public, and causing as much of a stink as I could, especially in the faces of the churches that are responsible.

It was on Vancouver Island just two weeks after our church occupation that life took a sudden and unusually pleasant change for me. Apparently the news of our audacious occupation had spread, and as a result I had been asked to speak at a community conference in Nanaimo. A hundred enthusiastic people received me at the hall that day, along with a young woman named Lori O'Rorke.

Life jumps out at us in strange ways, alternately clawing and caressing. That day, it was both unsuspected and a new departure. The woman I met would join her life to mine and fill a vacuum I had occupied for many years. Talking to her during an intermission, I realized that simply being together seemed to make sense to both of us.

Later we talked far into the night, beginning hesitantly to learn each other. Her passionate hatred of the injustice done to native and poor people meshed completely with the course I had mapped for myself. She had been an orphan herself, and was now a single mother and an instructor at Malaspina College in that city. Lori, I learned, had already read my website, and much of the material in my books.

In a word, she was hooked, and not just concerning my mission and the residential schools.

The following month, Lori organized a lecture for me at her college, and immediately began to experience the heat of associating with me. One woman, a member of the local United Church establishment, warned Lori to stay away from me. Why?

'Jim Manley gets very upset when Kevin's name is mentioned.'

Jim Manley was a local United Church minister and a former Member of Parliament. He had a long association with west coast missionaries, including such notables as Dr George Darby, a storied hero of the United Church's mission history. Among Darby's accomplishments, he had figured prominently in the program of sterilizing native women at Bella Bella, BC at his R.W. Large Hospital, which is still in operation.

'That Dr Darby took out my gold teeth when I was under anesthesia, and then he tied my tubes so I couldn't have any more children,' described Ethel Wilson at our IHRAAM Tribunal, back in 1998. But this kind of testimonial was simply made up, according to the likes of Mr Manley.

Apparently, my upsetting him and his guilty conscience was reason enough for Nanaimo citizens to shun me. But Lori wasn't fazed by the woman's comment, and asked what it was that I had done that was so wrong.

'He's making a career out of this residential school thing! And he isn't even native!' cried the woman.

'Do you have to be Jewish to oppose the Nazi Holocaust? Or Iraqi to oppose the war over there?' Lori replied adeptly, as the woman scurried off, red-faced.

Manley's defensiveness was more evidence that I was hitting all the right nerves, especially as Lori and I began to probe more deeply into other United Church operations, such as the local Nanaimo Indian Hospital, of which the remnant buildings still stood immediately to the south of Malaspina College.

At the meeting Lori organized, a native woman named Joan Morris stood up and described how she and her mother were kept confined in the Nanaimo Indian Hospital for more than thirteen years, despite the fact that neither of them had any illness.

'They kept giving me shots all the time, and some of the girls were fixed so they could never have children,' Joan described to the quiet audience.

'My cousin Nancy Joe and I were forced to eat this stuff that smelled like iodine. Nancy died of cancer when she was twenty-two, and I developed several tumors later. When I went to the doctor as an adult, he X-rayed me and said all the bones in my feet had been broken.'

Joan never was able to retrieve any of her medical records from her years in the Nanaimo Indian Hospital. Nor could her mother, or any of the other survivors of that hospital. There was a standard answer from the government: their files were a matter of national security, and couldn't be made public.

Kenny Quatell, who was also imprisoned in the Nanaimo hospital from the age of five until he was fourteen, was told by his doctor in Campbell River that he was part of a long-term study, but the doctor wouldn't elaborate.

In the late 1960s, Kenny was whisked from an operating table to the Nanaimo Indian Hospital, where he was given electric shocks and experimental drugs, put in sensory deprivation rooms, and experimented on daily for years. His parents were told that he had died on the operating table. He did not see them again until he was an adult.

'I can't remember how long they kept me in the dark room, but if I threw up the pills, they made me eat them again.'

I began to meet so many people like Kenny on Vancouver Island that I decided to move to Nanaimo, during 2004. Needless to say, Lori's being there was more than just another incentive. In that same year we began our life together, and we started documenting even more horrific stories from survivors all over Vancouver Island.

38
Spring 2005 – Vancouver Island
A Film is Born

I had been planning for a long time to produce a documentary film encompassing all of the stories and evidence of the crimes that had been shared with me, to tell the world the real story of the Indian residential schools. But no one with the technical expertise had ever shown any interest, and I never had more than two nickels to rub together.

Some time after I moved in with Lori an e-mail solved my problem. It came from someone called Louie Lawless. Initially, I wondered at the surname, thinking that it was some sort of practical joke. That was quickly dispelled, because Louie turned out to be a retired Hollywood director and film maker who wanted to speak to me. He lived an hour south of Nanaimo, in the town of Duncan, and had heard of me through the aboriginal grapevine.

I was prepared to be skeptical and for a time was reluctant to be disappointed. Thankfully, Louie was persistent. He eventually convinced Lori and me to meet him in Duncan.

Louie knew little about aboriginal people, as it turned out, but he had a nose for a story and he was fascinated by mine. Against my initial resistance, he succeeded in convincing me of the importance of what I had endured and learned.

'This story isn't about native people,' he insisted, looking at me across the table in the restaurant where we met. 'It's about you.'

He flogged me with his persistent Gaelic élan.

'It doesn't really register that there was genocide here. Most white people don't care, not that they're necessarily insensitive to it, but because they can't relate to it. What they can relate to is a white minister losing everything including his family and taking on his church and the establishment. People love a good David and Goliath story; and man, you've got one!'

This idea didn't sit well with me at all, and I almost told Louie to forget the whole thing. But fortunately, like Louie, Lori had grown up in rural British Columbia, and she knew what mainstream Canada thought of Indians. She agreed with Louie.

'What we need to do is to tell both stories,' Louie continued, 'yours and theirs. That's unique, combining both cultures like that. It'll be a bombshell!'

They finally convinced me. Before long, we were scripting what would become the first documentary film ever produced on the deeper truth of Canadian residential schools, not to mention what had happened to me.

It was Lori who came up with the title one night, in a flash of inspiration: *Unrepentant*.

'That describes both the church and you,' she observed seriously.

Filming *Unrepentant* took us about eighteen months, weaving together what had happened to me in Port Alberni and after, alternately with first-hand testimony from survivors of the residential schools and Indian hospitals, including people like Kenny Quatell.

The film was substantially based on the massive amount of material I had compiled in *Hidden from History*, thoroughly documenting the evidence proving the case that genocide in Canada had been planned and deliberate.

Louie was a consummate film maker and editor. He knew both how to frame the visuals and to force emotions out of me which I had thought were no longer there. He could see, even when I couldn't, that the world would be vitally interested in what had befallen me, simply because nothing is as compelling as one individual person opposing enormous forces, like Prometheus, like David, like Cuchulain's fight with the sea.

But there were several conflicts during the shooting, as Louie kept trying to force my real feelings out of me.

'Quit speaking from your head!' he'd yell at me as he and an assistant filmed me. 'Show me how you felt when they took your kids from you!'

Daily work on the film was not easy for me. Digging deeper into the memories and trauma of my firing, my divorce, and the horrors native people had shared with me over the years was painful in the extreme. But we kept at it, combining our new footage and interviews with survivors, material I'd gathered for seven or eight years.

The pain now surfacing was more than offset by the growing elation I felt that the full story would finally be out there, on film, for the world to see. I sensed that once people could see the living faces of the survivors, the whole story would take on flesh and blood and become much more real, even for non-natives. But never could I have imagined the explosive impact the film would have.

39
January 2007

In just a few months following its release, Unrepentant *wins two major awards at film festivals in New York and Los Angeles, is shown in hundreds of forums, and has received more than 50,000 hits on links widely disseminated on the internet, but more impressively it is in the top ranks of Google-posted videos. The film is copied and spreads like wildfire in communities across Canada.*

'This film puts us on the map for the very first time,' describes survivor Louis Daniels of Winnipeg to a national newspaper.

'You see the human face of the murder they did to our people. Now the world can't ignore us.'

There are two immediate indicators that at last the news is out, that Unrepentant *has shaken loose something in a hidden Canadian psyche of holocaust denial. Within a month of the film's release, major feature stories are published in the* Globe and Mail, *Canada's leading national daily, and in the* Ottawa Citizen, *all of which confirms what Kevin Annett has been stating for years: that over half of the children incarcerated in Indian residential schools died there.*

'Natives Died in Droves Despite Warning to Ottawa' trumpets newspaper headlines, mentioning the 50% death rate in Indian residential schools. Suddenly, for the first time since the 1998 Tribunal, Kevin Annett begins to receive phone calls from reporters, and is quoted in the national media.

The fact that his new network of supporters and survivors known as the Friends and Relatives of the Disappeared (FRD) has resumed occupations and protests at churches in Vancouver and Toronto helps to keep the media flame of interest burning, as he strategically plans the actions to coincide with the release of new evidence of mass graves of children near former residential schools.

Since 2005, Kevin and his core people within the FRD have observed a public 'Aboriginal Holocaust Memorial Day' on April 15 of each year, and have called on the Anglican, Roman Catholic and United Churches to surrender the remains of the children who died at their hands. This new focus on the missing children strikes a chord across Canada, especially as the April 15 memorial vigils spread to five other cities in addition to Vancouver, and the media begin reporting the event.

The second result, no doubt prompted by the FRD actions, is the naming of the crime in the Canadian Parliament for the first time.

Gary Merasty, a Member of the Liberal Party opposition in Canada's House of Commons, is also a former tribal council chief and member of the Cree Nation in northern Saskatchewan. In April of 2007, shortly after the release of Unrepentant, which he has seen, Merasty stands up in Parliament and asks the Minister of Indian Affairs, Jim Prentice, to start a process of repatriating the remains of the children who died in the residential schools.

Prentice responds that he will 'look into the missing children', and a new era begins in Canada. The Harper government is forced to announce the formation of a 'Missing Children's Task Force', and eventually, a misnamed 'Truth and Reconciliation Commission' (TRC) to enquire into the residential schools history.

Soon after speaking in Parliament, Gary Merasty resigns as a Member of Parliament after being hired by the uranium corporation Cameco in Saskatchewan to head their public relations department. Cameco had been in hot water with the local native bands over their practice of dumping contaminated uranium waste on their reserves.

As Brother Fidel in Chiapas observed, native leaders are not killed in

Canada, save a few like the patriot, Louis Riel. They for the most part continue to be placed on someone's payroll.

It is painfully apparent that there has not emerged so far a Martin Luther King among the indigenous people. On the one hand, there have been outstanding war leaders: Geronimo, Big Bear, Sitting Bull, Leonard Peltier, even, among the Metis, Louis Riel. Without exception they have either been executed or huddled with their people in some sterile wasteland deemed expendable by the pale paternal government.

Because of this, a new generation of native youth has of necessity emerged to fill the role abandoned by their elders. And it is this stratum of young and uncontained indigenous men and women who have become Kevin Annett's natural allies, who accompany him in church occupations and protests, and who still carry on the struggle to confront and change the face, and the heart and soul, of Canada from the grass-roots up.

40
2008–2009 – Canada

The wide release of *Unrepentant*, and the protests and media attention that followed in its wake, have been the key factor in prompting the Canadian government, and eventually Pope Benedict XVI in Rome, to address in some manner the crimes in the Indian residential schools of Canada. And that simple fact has been an enormous vindication for me and the many survivors who have stepped forward to tell the truth.

And yet...

Life in Canada is like walking through northern tundra. Beneath the blue and white vista, the beautiful snow-covered land, there lies a deep humus that can ensnare and kill. What you inhabit and traverse is unknowable until you fall through the thin crust, and discover what lies beneath.

At the same time that the state and church powers behind the genocide have been forced to grudgingly acknowledge some of their deeds – a significant victory – they have simultaneously exonerated themselves, silenced the witnesses, and tried desperately to isolate me and our work from the international support and exposure that they know will be their eventual undoing.

Under pressure from our campaign, the federal government announced the formation of a supposed 'Truth and Reconciliation Commission' (TRC) and made plans to 'apologize' officially for the sordid history of the residential schools. But, compared with the commission which had been its namesake in South Africa, which had been one of the engines that abolished apartheid, the Canadian TRC, as it turned out, would more closely resemble a church picnic than a Nuremburg.

Under its mandate, and in the typical Canadian manner of studying a problem at great expense rather than fixing it, the

TRC has no power to prosecute, to subpoena, or to lay criminal charges, against anyone. It cannot grant immunity to anyone testifying before it. Nor will it allow names of perpetrators to be named. And any wrongdoing in a residential school cannot be discussed, unless it was already dealt with in a court of law, which most of the crimes, and certainly homicide, have never experienced.

Such a sterile and self-serving body is hardly surprising, since the TRC Commissioners are nominated by the very churches the TRC is investigating!

If a single serial killer was allowed to name his jury, hobnob with the judge, and avoid prosecution and jail time by issuing verbal 'apologies' to his victims' families, such an obvious subversion of justice would come nowhere near the travesty being perpetrated by far more prolific killers: the Anglican, Catholic and United Church of Canada.

As important as it has been that the deaths and crimes are finally being acknowledged, nowhere in all of the growing rhetoric and mainstream coverage of the residential schools, nor in any government or church release, or in the subsequent 'apology' by Prime Minister Steven Harper, do the words 'blame', 'murder', 'trial', 'churches' or 'genocide' ever occur.

Nowhere in any government release, nor in the subsequent 'apology', nor in any action ever taken by any of the major church organizations, do the words 'indict', 'trial', or especially 'murder' occur. Indeed, shortly after the TRC was announced, it was also stated by the government that 'no criminal charges would be laid', despite the fact that criminal acts occurred in the residential schools.

'Healing fund', yes. 'Reconciliation', incessantly, along with that perennial church bromide 'outreach'. But no mention that in 120 years not a single person has ever been brought to trial for the death of a single child in a Canadian Indian residential school.

No 'M' word: it is not in our lexicon. It never happened,

officially. We have experienced the greatest crime in our history, yet one officially devoid of criminals.

If they could, the pale lawyers and politicians and bishops who drone on about 'apologies' to their victims should listen, and attentively, to the thoughts of the late Chief Joseph of the Nez Perce Nation (1840–1904):

> Words do not pay for my dead people. They do not pay for my country now overrun by white men. They do not protect my Father's grave. They do not pay for my horses and cattle. Good words cannot give me back my children. Good words will not give my people good health and stop them from dying. Good words will not give my people a good home where they can live in peace and take care of themselves. I am tired of talk that comes to nothing. It makes my heart sick when I remember all the good words and all the broken promises. There has been too much talking by men who have no right to talk.

I am haunted by the vision of Maisie Shaw, and more than 50,000 other children. The real question is, why is not the rest of Canada equally haunted?

41
August 2009 – East Side,
Vancouver, Canada

For the protagonist of this unfinished saga, there is neither final victory, nor defeat, but ultimately only the people: the ones he was first called to serve decades before, in a place not far from where he now sits, in the Ovaltine Café on East Hastings Street.

The grinding ambiguity of his existence is clarified as always by speaking with the witnesses, the ones who understand, and who bring the only reassurance to the man he has ever known for years, and that is the truth itself.

He sits that morning in the warm familiarity of the greasy spoon known for its depression-era wooden booths, a feature which is so popular among the film companies that use the neighborhood like the middle-class johns who drive around every night, looking for young native prostitutes. Sheila Little walks in and joins him.

Sheila is a native woman living in exile from her northern coastal people, in the downtown east side of Vancouver – a free-fire zone for Indians, where dozens disappear every year from 'starlight tours' at the hands of people who may be police, or otherwise for hire, or simply practitioners of random racist murder.

Sheila has fled from her traditional territory because of attempts to kill her and her children in order to gain their land. In fact, she is a clan mother, one of a group that Kevin's people and government has tried to wipe out, through murder, sterilization, and legal eradication. And, in their matrilineal society, her daughter was in line to inherit their land – and that land was hungrily sought by forest companies.

Sheila first contacted Kevin in 2001.

'I've a lot to tell you,' she wrote. 'I've heard I can talk about these things with you.'
She was assaulted and nearly killed after that, and has been in hiding ever since. Only now, eight years later, has she emerged,

Sheila pauses, and squints at the slight and unassuming man.
'I thought you'd be bigger.'
Over a rare meal, Sheila begins to talk.

'When I was not even twelve, I got pregnant from a priest at the Mission residential school. When they found out, they gave me a drug and tied me to a bed. They did something to make the baby come out. All that time, the nuns were saying it was an unholy child and had to die. Later on, I learned they had buried the baby in the field next to the school after drowning it in a bucket of water.

'The same thing happened to my sister Bernice when she got raped by a priest there. Her baby disappeared and she never saw it again.'
Sheila stops, tears in her eyes, and looks at Kevin coldly.

'I ran away from that place after that. Me and two boys, Dennis and Walter. We got caught pretty quick, somebody ratted on us. So we had to go back to the school.

They locked up Dennis in a broom closet for two weeks for running away, and they never fed him much. They beat him pretty bad. When I ran into him last year in Terrace, he looked like an old, old man. He broke down and started crying as soon as he saw me.'
Kevin is scribbling away on a napkin but looks up when she begins to cry.

'Our top chief, he sold off 20,000acres of his people's land, all illegally

without anyone knowing. The company gave him a new house, a new fishing boat, three new cars. Anyone who objected got a one-way ride to the lake and disappeared.

My whole family has been killed off so that we don't inherit our land. The chief made sure of that so that his friends in the logging company can get it all.'

She declines to name either the chief or the logging company, for she wants to live to see her grandchildren. But their identities are obvious, and much quoted in the press.

Later, Sheila describes all the young native men she knows who have been 'taken for a ride' by the city police of Terrace and Prince George during sub-zero weather, and have never returned.

'They take them twenty, thirty miles outside of town and dump them there, all the time. It happened to my nephew Bobby and his buddy just after we got there. Two cops pulled over where they were sitting at a bus stop and forced them into the car. It was twenty below zero that night. They dumped them an hour outside of town. They would have died that night but somebody spotted them and brought them back.

'The cops do that to our people all the time. That's just normal around there. It's why we say the residential schools never closed for us.'

The protagonist nods, having heard the same story so many times. He puts away his notes and looks at Sheila, waiting, wondering what will come next, for either of them. Strangely, they both know the answer, but they do not say what they know, out of concern for the other.

42
The Present Time – On the Requiem Road

A week before my first child Clare was born in a North Bay, Ontario hospital, I was present with Donovan Mick when he died, at the side of his grieving wife of seventy-one years, Edith. I was interning for the ministry then, but had never seen anyone die before my eyes.

Edith and I were both holding Donovan's thin, withered hands that cold January morning, as his strong will kept forcing his cancer-ravaged body to breathe again, and again. His eyes flickered open, and I could see he was about to go. The piercing blue orbs sought Edith, and turned to his beloved and embraced her a final time. He smiled at her briefly. And then he vanished.

My heart rather than my eyes saw the portal open just then, and felt the rush of purity fill the room and flood us with radiance. I saw a gateway to forever open, and then close. And I turned, and saw in Edith's joyful gaze that she had seen it, too.

On January 22, 1989, an identical radiance broke through the same, brief doorway when my firstborn Clare Rose spilled forth into our world. I felt and saw the portal again, and the forever, as my child opened her eyes and looked carefully at her father, and we knew each other instantly. As Anne and I wept and embraced, and held our newborn daughter, I believed for the first time in my life that love, our word for the radiance and the forever, is the only actual reality; and that all else is transitory illusion.

To die is to return to reality, said my Celtic ancestors, and they were right. For in death we discover what is real: the eternal moment whose nature is love, and which stands outside time and decay. And so it is with no regrets that I have learned over fifteen years to accept the reality of my own death at the hands of violent men who robbed me of my old life, my children, and my secure attachment to a world of lies. For that death has ushered me into that 'realm of eternity' that Jesus spoke of, and which was falsely translated in the Bible as 'the kingdom of God'.

'The realm of eternity is within you, and among you, and around you,' reads Jesus' words in his original Aramaic tongue – and not in the church, he might have added, if he was alive today to see how Christianity has so violated and denied him. That realm is everywhere, but we don't see it, mostly – not until death and ending brings its possibility closer to us.

When it does approach, the eternal realm allows us to see all things as they are, which is limitless, and the boundaries, concepts and rules which are all illusion burst and float away, and our natural unity with all things returns. It is only then that we can know who we really are, and what we are to do.

What seemed to me at first to be the unending and meaningless suffering of persecution was actually my entry route to this eternal state, and my acquiring of an understanding that our time as a people and a culture is over.

The signs of our ending are everywhere, but death is something that our dissociated selves fear and hide from, and we can only deny the obvious – even when we breathe it and walk through it every day. Like a delirious terminal cancer patient, our culture can only rave about how we'll be on our feet any day now, once the right cure is found. But there is no cure for what we have become, and for the death that awaits us.

I have learned that the extermination my people inflicted on indigenous nations for centuries began against ourselves, long before, in Europe, and under the banner of religion and faith. When I journeyed to Italy in October 2009, after my vigil outside the Vatican I met a small cluster of Waldensi Christians in Parma, the descendants of early Protestant dissidents whose ancestors, like my own Huguenot forebears in France, somehow survived the slaughter foisted on them by the Catholic Church. Suddenly, I knew myself to be, like the residential school natives, a survivor of genocide. And I knew that the same crime of self-assured conquest of 'the Other' is not only continuing, but is threatening to destroy our sacred planet.

The natural world lies fallow every few years, to renew and replenish the earth; and all that once grew must die for the new life to begin. All cultures follow the same cycle, and in these last days, as our ecosystems shudder and fail, and reason and hope vanish under police state brutality, we have come face to face with what has caused our ending, and that is the same force that murdered and sterilized innocent aboriginal children in the name of our jealous and murderous god Jehovah, and that continues to deny and hide the truth.

And yet the eternal realm that is imperishable, and is within us, will outlive the present ending, but only if we heed the prophecy given to our people by the teacher we have so rejected, who said that the spirit of eternity is upon each of us, and calls us to set the captives free, and bring sight to the blind, and proclaim the Jubilee liberation when society will lie fallow, and all things are returned to their natural state.

And so it's time, finally, to lay down everything, dear reader, and withdraw from the social disorder that calls itself 'civilization'. The institutions have fallen, whether of church or state, and since it is the dead who should certainly bury the dead, it is up to you, the living, to recover your life from the dull technological slavery that you've been taught to subsist in. And no one can do that for you.

One of my best friends died just recently, as I finish writing these lines in the early weeks of 2010. His name was Bingo Dawson, a homeless aboriginal man who stood bravely in our front ranks whenever we occupied a church and demanded justice for the living and the dead. Bingo was beaten mercilessly by three Vancouver policemen just days before he died, and that attack probably killed him. But as an anonymous graffiti message scrawled on the corner where Bingo lived tells us,

'Bingo: from friend to angel. This is still your corner forever.'

Bingo, like Donovan Mick and Maisie Shaw and Harriet Nahanee and countless others, make me that much stronger now that they stand firmly in the realm of eternity, where love presides, pure and unalloyed; and where all partialness and corruption is gone. They stand that close to us all, and we to them; and into that stream of eternity I dip every day.

Let us struggle and survive, oh my people.

43
Recessional – A Pyrrhic Victory

It ends as it began. Except that now it is winter in Port Alberni, and Christmas Eve. Some sixty-five years have passed since that other Christmas Eve, when Maisie Shaw lay dying on a cold basement floor. Above, Alfred Caldwell, who put her there, led the children in singing of the birth of Jesus on the same night that he killed her. Unlike Maisie, he would die peacefully in his bed, and be lauded in official accounts.

The sound of caroling is wafted across the Alberni inlet, to hover over the graves of Maisie Shaw and so many other slaughtered innocents. Snow is falling gently on their graves, like a benediction.

It has been, one journalist writes, a Pyrrhic victory. A victory at enormous, perhaps prohibitive, cost. And perhaps equally questionable, whose victory is it?

The Empire Church has not toppled, at least not in appearance. Overbearing and ponderous, like a great ocean liner, it sails on, although sagging now as its lower levels fill with seawater from irremediable damage. For now, its dogma remains, its massive corporate structure as rigid as ever, although teetering, its doctrinal encyclicals more redolent than ever of confident Christian supremacy.

The government remains remote, austere and untouchable. Those in power will no more judge and convict themselves than an American President will indict or try a former administration, should antecedent crime ever be discovered.

The proper agenda, right there for all to see on the order paper, has been observed. If there have indeed been two centuries of official malfeasance, of colonial tyranny, of official denial; if thousands of tiny souls have been extinguished as a practical necessity, then that has been ostensibly recognized and erased by a parliamentary apology, accompanied by monetary crumbs issued by the Ministry of Supply.

The Royal Canadian Mounted Police, it will continue to be taught in the elementary schools, was founded in 1873 by a grateful although indifferent Queen Victoria. The Force fought valiantly to quell native uprisings at Duck Lake and Cypress Hills, and it even put down Louis Riel, the Metis rebel. Riel, although elected a Member of Parliament by his constituents, was hanged by the neck until dead, as had already happened to the Cree medicine man Wandering Spirit, for the same reason.

And at about the same time, the proud Force's sole participation in the residential school saga was simply that, in the finest tradition of the Empire, they took their marching orders from higher up: a legal precedent that serves to exonerate all government subordinates, despite what was said at Nuremburg.

The media, most recently, have finally found it advantageous and permissible to tell the astonishing story of a now not-so-young firebrand, as if it has just happened and is therefore newsworthy. They write excitedly that he has, like a professional rodeo rider, bitten the establishment's ear for seventeen years now. As one more adventurous journalist says:

'Kevin Annett is a modern day David who may not have whipped old Goliath, but he did hit the s.o.b. a pretty good lick between the eyes.'
What of the protagonist?

Perhaps he can still hear the sounds that count as he talks with his people in Oppenheimer Park in the downtown east side of Vancouver, those who by some odd twist of faith or decision, became his real congre-

gation – those who now, in the winter of their suffering, have only strips of cardboard for shelter.

Perhaps it is enough for him that he treasures the name of Eagle Strong Voice given him by Chief Louis Daniels of the Anishinabe Nation when he was honored by that nation with adoption. And that he recalls most humbly the Lakota prediction:

'In our time there will come among us a white man who will give us a voice.'
Perhaps all temporal wars, all battles, end in Pyrrhic victories, for either side: too costly to warrant a sense of triumph.

Still, he cannot find the conviction to believe that all has been for naught. The snow, the benediction, is still falling on the unmarked graves, and the music from some blithely unaware organist is now audible. It speaks of an ideal never lived, but always tantalizing and subversive, beckoning to those who would dare to embody and follow its sacrificial light.

He is drawn by that light to where this story began, indeed where the crime originated, in the place of the Lost Ideal, outside the Edifice in Rome where he summoned the truth, and a tornado, to make the message manifest. To that symbol of all that is twisted and betrayed in our world, and in ourselves, he will return, time and again: no longer alone, but in the company of all those who can live no longer alongside the Lie that huddles under the Emperor's robes.

It is enough that he has come this far. It is enough to have been sifted and refined in the hands of the Great Mystery.

BOOKS

O is a symbol of the world, of oneness and unity. In different cultures it also means the "eye," symbolizing knowledge and insight. We aim to publish books that are accessible, constructive and that challenge accepted opinion, both that of academia and the "moral majority."

Our books are available in all good English language bookstores worldwide. If you don't see the book on the shelves ask the bookstore to order it for you, quoting the ISBN number and title. Alternatively you can order online (all major online retail sites carry our titles) or contact the distributor in the relevant country, listed on the copyright page.

See our website www.o-books.net for a full list of over 500 titles, growing by 100 a year.

And tune in to myspiritradio.com for our book review radio show, hosted by June-Elleni Laine, where you can listen to the authors discussing their books.

MySpiritRadio